AHMED BELKAOUI
University of Ottawa

CONCEPTUAL FOUNDATIONS OF MANAGEMENT ACCOUNTING

ADDISON-WESLEY PUBLISHING COMPANY
Reading, Massachusetts • Menlo Park, California
London • Amsterdam • Don Mills, Ontario • Sydney

This book is in the
Addison-Wesley Paperback Series in Accounting

Consulting Editor
William J. Bruns, Jr.

Library of Congress Cataloging in Publication Data

Belkaoui, Ahmed, 1943-
Conceptual foundations of management accounting.

(Paperback series in accounting)
Bibliography: p.
Includes index.
1. Managerial accounting. I. Title.
HF5635.B4168 658.1'511 80-16086
ISBN 0-201-00097-0 (pbk.)

Library of Congress Catalog Card No. 80-16086.

ISBN 0-201-00097-0
ABCDEFGHIJ-DO-89876543210

...DATIONS OF ...CCOUNTING

To Janice

EDITOR'S FOREWORD

The environment for accounting has undergone revolutionary changes in the last decade. Demand for accountability by managers of both public and private organizations has risen significantly. Electronic data transmission, storage, and processing and other information technologies have developed to allow accountants to use methods and processes that would have been considered impossible, or uneconomical, just a few years ago. At the same time, new quantitative methods for solving accounting problems have been developed, and the behavioral sciences have suggested that the impact of accounting goes well beyond the systems and reports which are the most visible product of the accountant's work.

The speed with which these developments have occurred has made it difficult for teachers and students of accounting, and for managers and accountants themselves, to keep their knowledge up-to-date. New solutions to problems, and sometimes even new kinds of accounting problems themselves, are not treated in many textbooks. In addition, problems and solutions often cross boundaries between what were once considered separate disciplines of study. The student or manager seeking a learning aid in an era of change will frequently be frustrated. In many respects, materials which have been available do not reflect either the new developments or the unprecedented opportunities for creative thinking and problem solving which accounting presents.

Each book in this Addison-Wesley Series treats a new development or subject which has not been widely treated in textbooks which are widely available. In addition, because each book concentrates on a single set of problems, methods, or topics in accounting, each provides comprehensive coverage in an economical form. The Series was conceived to help all who work with or process accounting information, all of whom must continue to learn in order to keep pace with the changes which are occurring. Each book has been carefully developed by an outstanding scholar.

Books in this Series were prepared in the belief that the evaluation of accounting and its importance to managers will continue, and with faith that books are an effective means to assist all who are interested to participate in the developments which will take place in the future. Our goal has been to improve the practice and processes of accounting, and to help all who use accounting information to do so more effectively.

William J. Bruns, Jr.
Professor of Business Administration
Harvard University

CONTENTS

PREFACE

This book is designed to provide additional material for a typical course in management accounting. The student in management accounting should be aware not only of the new multidisciplinary scope of the field but also of the conceptual foundations which justify this extended scope. Most management accounting texts do not introduce and integrate all these foundations and are generally restricted to an exposition of cost accounting techniques. In my judgment, what is needed is to show the student that management accounting has a conceptual grounding in various disciplines, justifying the adaptation of their techniques to managerial problem solving. It is to this view of management accounting that this book is addressed.

Four conceptual foundations envisioned for management accounting are presented: Accounting foundations (Chapter 1); Organizational foundations (Chapter 2); Behavioral foundations (Chapter 3); and Decisional foundations (Chapter 4). A recurrent theme in each of these chapters is that a failure to grasp any of these conceptual foundations of management accounting may result in deficiencies in the management accounting system and inadequacies in the provision of the diverse services required by both the small and the complex organizations of today.

I wish to acknowledge Professors Martin Bariff and William J. Bruns, Jr., who made valuable comments. The manuscript was written when I was spending a sabbatical at the Graduate School of Business at the University of Chicago. I especially thank Sylvia Dobray, Jane Hilmers, Constance Hunt, and the typists of the Faculty Secretarial Service in that institution for their cheerful and intelligent assistance.

Ottawa, Canada A. B.
May 1980

Introduction

CONCEPTUAL FOUNDATIONS OF MANAGEMENT ACCOUNTING

Accounting foundations

Organizational foundations

Behavioral foundations

Decisional foundations

Management accounting is designed, first, to supply information to internal decision makers of a given organization, second, to facilitate their decision making, third, to motivate their actions and behavior in a desirable direction and, finally, to promote the efficiency of the organization. It is accounting-based and individual-, organization-, and decision-centered. Thus, management accounting requires an accounting, behavioral, organizational, and decisional grounding. An understanding of each of these foundations may allow the management accountant to design a management accounting system responsive to the diverse needs and demands emanating from within and from without the organization. A failure to grasp any of these foundations, as they pertain to either the accounting discipline, the individual, the organization, or the decision, may result in deficiencies in the management accounting system and failures to adequately provide diverse services required by both small and complex organizations.

The book has four major themes corresponding to the four conceptual foundations envisioned for management accounting. Without attempting to summarize the entire book, here are a few brief overview comments on each of the conceptual foundations of management accounting.

Accounting foundations

The accounting characteristic or problem of management accounting is one of determining the ways in which accounting information may be accumulated, classified, analyzed, and adapted to specific problems, decisions, and day-to-day conduct of an organization. These management accounting techniques should be derived and supported by a management accounting conceptual framework. Chapter 1 of this book shows that an emerging management accounting conceptual framework exists with the identification in the literature of its required elements; namely, the objectives, qualitative characteristics, concepts, and techniques of management accounting.

Organizational foundations

The organizational characteristic or problem of management accounting is one of tailoring the internal reporting system to the organizational structure and to the significant elements which approximate the patterning and order inherent in organizations. This objective requires a good understanding of the elements of organization structure and the theories of organization. Chapter 2 discusses the elements of organization structure that may affect the ways the management function will be exercised, including the nature of the organization, the organization structure or hierarchy, the line and staff relationships, and the functions of the controller. The theories of organization that point to significant elements which approximate the patterning or order existing in organizations and define the ways management accounting will better provide its services include the rational perspective, the classical perspective, the human relations perspective, and the natural systems perspective.

Behavioral foundations

The behavioral characteristic or problem of management accounting is one of adapting the internal reporting system to the different factors that shape the "cognitive make-up" of individuals within the organization and affect their performance. These factors include the perception by the individual of what should be the objective function or goals of the firm, the various elements likely to motivate the individual to perform, and the decision-making model most relevant to particular contexts and most preferred by the individual. As seen in Chapter 3, the objective function may be either a stockholder wealth maximization, a managerial welfare maximization, or a social welfare maximization. The factors that may motivate the individual to perform are specified by the different motivation theories; namely, the need theory, the two-factor theory, the value/expectancy theory, the achievement theory, and the inequity theory.

Finally, the individual may adopt as a decision-making model the rational view, the satisficing process-oriented view, the organizational procedures view, the political view, or the individual differences view. Each of these behavioral concepts identify factors and situations that influence the individual behavior, and indicate avenues for management accounting to adapt its services.

Decisional foundations

The decisional characteristic or problem of management accounting is one of determining the types of decision and decision systems, the type of information and information system needed. Several frameworks have been proposed in the literature for viewing these decisional foundations, namely, the Anthony framework, Simon framework, Gorry-Scott Morton framework, Forrester framework, Dearden framework, and Blumenthal framework. Each of these frameworks, discussed in Chapter 4, provides the basis for making resource allocation decisions about information systems in general and management accounting in particular.

Chapter One

THE ACCOUNTING FOUNDATIONS

Management accounting is one of the areas in the field and profession of accountancy. As suggested by the 1958 American Accounting Association (AAA) Committee on Management Accounting, it "involves consideration of the ways in which accounting information may be accumulated, synthesized, analyzed, and presented in relation to specific problems, decisions, and day-to-day tasks of business management."[1] An appreciation of management accounting requires a good understanding of the different facets of accounting in organizations. A clarification of each of the areas of accounting will help identify the scope of management accounting, the possibility of a management accounting theory, and a taxonomy of management accounting techniques.

The aim of this chapter is to clarify the role of management accounting in the field of accounting per se, and argue for a management accounting theory as a frame of reference for the justification of present and new management accounting techniques.

1.1 NATURE OF ACCOUNTING

The financial community has always regarded the accounting discipline as one of its principal tools in the decision-making process. The primacy of decision has been stressed by both Paton and the "Statement of Basic Accounting Theory":

> The purpose of accounting may be said to be that of interpreting the financial data . . . to provide a sound guide action by management, investor and other interested parties.[2]
>
> The committee defines accounting as the process of identifying, measuring, and communicating economic information to permit informed judgments and decisions by users of the information.[3]

Thus, accounting is perceived as utilitarian in purpose and descriptive in nature. Stated in means-end terms, the end sought is good information, the means employed are descriptions. Accounting provides information for two distinct but closely related purposes: (1) making decisions within the organization; and, (2) reporting to persons outside the organization who have a legitimate interest in its affairs.

The first reporting scheme is the area of internal or management accounting, the second is the area of external or financial accounting. What is the extent of the differences in scope of both financial and management accounting?

1.2 FINANCIAL VERSUS MANAGEMENT ACCOUNTING

Financial accounting deals with reporting information that pertains to the financial position, performance, and conduct of a firm for a given period to a set of users and the market in general. Management accounting is more oriented toward internal decision making and purposively channels relevant and timely information to internal managers. Both are production processes of different accounting data for different problem-solving situations.

Financial accounting is the result of applying generally accepted accounting principles to the recording of transactions between different entities. As such, financial accounting statements conform to a set of rules established by the profession. Management accounting, however, reflects the use of techniques from different disciplines, including accounting, for internal problem solving. Therefore, management accounting techniques may differ from generally accepted accounting techniques, and from one firm to another. They do not conform to any set of prescribed rules, and much may be left to the decision-maker's philosophies.

In short, the frame of reference used in management accounting is much broader than that used in financial accounting. Boyd and Taylor considered the specific difference to be the following:

1. The managerial approach places the student in the role of a *user* of financial data in decision making. The conventional approach assigns the student the role of *preparer* of financial statements for use by others.
2. The student of managerial accounting is called upon to use his entire knowledge of the business world in making business decisions based upon accounting data. Conventional accounting limits itself to accounting techniques, principles, and practices, and rarely deals with decisions other than those required in the preparation of financial statements.
3. An attempt is made to consider the external and internal business environment in managerial accounting. Conventional accounting usually ignores these conditions.
4. The arrangement and emphasis of topical material differs under the two methods because of the differences in objectives.
5. The purpose of managerial accounting is to make a decision related to a business problem. Conventional accounting has as its end the ability to prepare adequate financial statements.[4]

To this list of differences, it may be also added that financial accounting data are required to be objective and verifiable, while management accounting emphasizes relevance and flexibility.

1.3 MANAGEMENT VERSUS COST ACCOUNTING

Although the relationship between cost accounting and management accounting has not been explicitly clarified, it is usually believed that it is one of point of emphasis. Cost accounting deals mainly with cost accumulation, inventory valuation, and product costing. It emphasizes the cost side. The objective function is implicitly perceived to be cost minimization. Similarly, management accounting deals with the efficient allocation of resources.

The objective function may be perceived to be profit maximization.[5] It is also believed that the cost accountant and the management accountant are performing different activities; cost control is in the domain of the cost accountant, while cost reduction is in the domain of the management accountant.[6] A cursory examination of accounting textbooks shows that, in general, those labeled *cost accounting* emphasize cost control, while those labeled *management accounting* or *managerial accounting* emphasize planning, which may have reinforced the belief in a difference of scope between both areas.[7] It is advisable, however, not to stress those differences, but rather to conceive of management accounting as an attempt to bring techniques from other disciplines into the area of cost accounting. In fact, in recent years, the scope of cost accounting has been enlarged in various ways:

1. It emphasizes not only the explanatory but also the predictive ability of accounting data.
2. It develops normative models to be applied in the accounting context with an emphasis on mathematical, statistical, and operations research techniques.
3. It stresses the behavioral impact of accounting information on the users.
4. It uses nonaccounting information, economic, environmental, and qualitative information to improve the relevance of management accounting data.
5. It merges economic and social goals and consequently draws the accountant into program budgets and "performance" auditing in not-for-profit organizations.
6. It relies on more frequent and heavier use of computers, leading to a centralization of information and the expected candidature of the management accountant for the job of the "information manager" having overall responsibility of this resource.

This enlargement of the scope of cost accounting into management accounting leads to the problem of the modern education of management accountants, which can either be resolved by an exposure of students to a proliferation of courses in the computer, quantitative, and behavioral sciences, or to an integrated multidisciplinary approach as advocated in this monograph. Following the same line of reasoning, the 1972 AAA Committee on Courses in Managerial Accounting made the following appropriate assumptions:

1. The role of managerial accounting encompasses the entire formalized information function of an organization.
2. The accountant is the best candidate for a manager of this information system.
3. Managerial accounting should be developed around a framework for the information-resource which will enhance an organization-wide perspective in the analysis and design of the information function.
4. Managerial accounting should integrate material from the computer, the quantitative, and the behavioral sciences areas.
5. Management accounting should continue the traditional emphasis on problems while using more sophisticated approaches to problem solving.[8]

In brief, management accounting should go beyond cost accounting and integrate various material from organization theory, behavioral sciences, information theory, etc., in a multidisciplinary approach aimed at facilitating the production of information for internal decision making. In spite of these diversifications in the background of management accountants, they remain professionals, as evidenced by the growing popularity of the *Certificate in Management Accounting* program of the National Association of Accountants (NAA). The following excerpt from a brochure issued by the NAA highlights the new scope of the management accountant's activities:

> More and more people—inside the business world and out—realize the significant changes which have been taking place for years

in accounting and the role of the accountant in business. No longer is he simply a recorder of business history. He now plays a dynamic role in making business decisions, in future planning and in almost every aspect of business operations. This new accountant is called a Management Accountant and he sits with top management because his key responsibility is developing, producing and analyzing information to help management make sound decisions. Many management accountants make their way to top management positions.

In response to the needs of business and at the request of many in the academic community, the National Association of Accountants has established a program to recognize professional competence in this field—a program leading to the certificate in Management Accounting.

The CMA program requires candidates to pass a series of uniform examinations and meet specific educational and professional standards to qualify for and maintain the Certificate in Management Accounting. NAA has established the Institute of Management Accounting to administer the program, conduct the examinations and grant certificates to those who qualify.

The objectives of the program are threefold: (1) to establish management accounting as a recognized profession by identifying the role of the management accountant and the underlying body of knowledge, and by outlining a course of study by which such knowledge can be acquired; (2) to foster higher educational standards in the field of management accounting; (3) to assist employers, educators and students by establishing objective measurement of an individual's knowledge and competence in the field of management accounting.

1.4 MANAGEMENT ACCOUNTING THEORY

Management accounting is generally understood as referring to the use of techniques. For example, the 1958 Committee on Management Accounting (CMA) defines it as:

> . . . the application of appropriate techniques and concepts in processing the historical and projected economic data of an en-

> tity to assist management in establishing a plan for reasonable economic objectives, and in the making of rational decisions with a view towards achieving these objectives.[9]

One may ask if these techniques are supported by a management accounting theory.

A generally accepted definition of a theory, as it could apply to management accounting, is that a theory represents "the coherent set of hypothetical, conceptual and pragmatic principles for a field of inquiry."[10] Accordingly, management accounting theory may be defined as a frame of reference in the form of a set of postulates and/or principles from different disciplines by which management accounting techniques are evaluated. The task of justifying the existence of a management accounting theory lies in the definition of appropriate postulates and principles. Given the differences in the objectives between management accounting and financial accounting, the postulates of financial accounting, with some exceptions, do not hold true for management accounting. In fact, the 1961 AAA Management Accounting Committee, charged with determining the relevance of financial accounting concepts to management accounting, concluded that (1) the concepts underlying internal reporting differ in several important respects from those of external public reporting; (2) these differences are due to differences in the objectives of both areas; and (3) it is justified to develop a separate body of concepts applicable to internal reporting.[11]

There is a need, then, for the accounting profession to develop a conceptual framework in management accounting to guide the development and use of techniques. Similar to financial accounting, such a framework would include the following elements:

1. The *objectives* of management accounting as the first and important step for the development of the elements of the conceptual framework for management accounting.

2. *Qualitative characteristics* to be met as essential attributes of management accounting information.
3. *Management accounting concepts* as the foundation for the body of knowledge contained within the conceptual framework.
4. *Management accounting techniques* and procedures which constitute the internal accounting systems.

Although these elements and the total integrated framework have not yet been formalized through a deductive reasoning process, they do exist in the literature as separate attempts to resolve these issues. Each of the proposed elements of management accounting will be examined next.

1.4.1 Objectives of management accounting

The objectives of management accounting are the first and essential step to the formulation of a management accounting theory. Then, the management accounting concepts will be true because they will be based on accepted objectives. In spite of the importance of management accounting objectives, there has never been a formal attempt by the profession to accomplish such a task. One noticeable exception, which may serve as *de facto* objectives of management accounting, was provided by the 1972 AAA Committee on Courses in Managerial Accounting. Four objectives were presented:

A. Management accounting should be related to the planning functions of the managers. This involves:
   1. Goal identification.
   2. Planning for optimal resource flows and their measurement.

B. Management accounting should be related to organizational problem areas. This includes:
   1. Relating the structure of the firm to its goals.
   2. Installing and maintaining an effective communication and reporting system.

3. Measuring existing resource uses, discovering exceptional performance, and identifying causal factors of such exceptions.

C. Management accounting should be related to the management control function. This includes:
1. Determining economic characteristics of appropriate performance areas which are significant in terms of overall goals.
2. Aiding to motivate desirable individual performances through a realistic communication of performance information in relation to goals.
3. Highlighting performance measures indicating goal incongruity within identifiable performance and responsibility areas.

D. Management accounting should be related to operating systems management, by function, product, project, or other segmentation of operations. This involves:
1. Measurement of relevant cost input and/or revenue or statistical measures of outputs.
2. Communication of appropriate data, of essentially economic character, to critical personnel on a timely basis.[12]

While these objectives reflect some of the priorities facing management accounting, they do not represent all the facets of the environment of management accounting. A formal study for the objectives of management accounting is a definite must for the profession.

1.4.2 Qualitative characteristics of management accounting information

Management accounting information should have certain desirable properties so that benefits are achievable. The 1969 American Accounting Association Committee on Managerial Decision Models explored the application to internal reporting of the standards of relevance, verifiability, freedom from bias, and quantifiability.[13] These standards for accounting information were those suggested in the *AAA Statement of Basic Accounting Theory*.[14] This effort was pursued by the 1974 AAA Committee on Concepts and Standards—Internal Planning and Control.[15] The Committee offered the following closely related properties as representatives of the benefits information or information systems:

1. Relevance/mutuality of objectives
2. Accuracy/precision/reliability
3. Consistency/comparability/uniformity
4. Verifiability/objectivity/neutrality/traceability
5. Aggregation
6. Flexibility/adaptability
7. Timeliness
8. Understandability/acceptability/motivation/fairness[16]

The findings of thc Committee are discussed next.

1. *Relevance/mutuality of objectives.* Relevant information is that which bears upon or is useful to "the action it is designed to facilitate or the result it is desired to produce."[17] For example, given different alternatives, the relevant costs and revenues are those expected costs and revenues which will be different for at least one of the alternatives. Historical costs may only be the basis for estimating expected future costs.

Relevance depends on the structure of the objective function. In other words, relevant information is the information on any variables in the user's objective function and must be very close to the definition implicit in the objective function. Relevance is a qualitative rather than a quantitative characteristic in the sense that information is either relevant or not.

Finally, relevance depends on the particular user receiving the information and on his or her particular decision. Some variables may be relevant to one user and not to others, and to one type of decision and not to others.

Mutuality of objectives refers to the consistency and congruency of the goals of the information users with those established by top management for the whole organization. The information provided by the internal reporting system may contribute to internal goal congruency if the signals of success or failure have the same meaning for both the total organization and its different segments. The mutuality of objectives applies also to the management accountants or the "internal information processors." Their goals should be consistent with the organizational goals.

2. *Accuracy/precision/reliability*. These properties are statistically interrelated in the sense that the notion of accuracy is statistically expressed by the concepts of precision and reliability. The specification of precision requires the specification of reliability, and vice versa.[18] Cyert and Davidson define these concepts as follows:

> . . . reliability is commonly used to describe the chances that a confidence interval will contain the true value being estimated . . . precision is often used in describing the interval about a sample estimate.[19]

While it is generally impossible to reach 100-percent accuracy, it is advisable to specify upper and lower bounds within which accuracy may be an effective property of management accounting information.

3. *Consistency/comparability/uniformity*. Consistency refers to the continued use of the same rules and procedures by the same firm over time, leading to comparability of its own statements with each other from one year to another. Uniformity refers to the use of similar rules by different firms. Consistency, uniformity, and the ensuing comparability are considered desirable criteria for financial accounting. Their relevance to management accounting differs between long-term and short-term decisions. A long-range planning decision relies on diverse, un-

structured information and nonrepetitive situations, and it may be unduly hampered by an internal accounting system stressing consistency/comparability/uniformity. However, the areas of short-run planning and performance control rely more on carefully structured information and repetitive situations, and lend themselves to an internal accounting system stressing consistency/comparability/uniformity.

4. *Verifiability/objectivity/neutrality/traceability.* Verifiability and objectivity refer to measurements that can be duplicated by independent measurers using the same measurement methods. It is usually operationally measured by the dispersion of the data in terms of the variance of the data. If the measurement rules are well specified, the verifiability of the measurement may be accomplished through a reconstruction of the initial measurement process and on the basis of evidential documents referred to as the audit trail. Traceability refers to the availability of such an audit trail. Finally, neutrality refers to the impartiality of the data in terms of its impact on different groups. A personal interest of the measurer in the data will not likely lead to neutral measurements. The degree of verifiability/objectivity/traceability of the data generated for management accounting is not as pronounced as when applied to financial accounting. However, neutrality of the information is a desirable objective, especially when the data are used for information evaluation or as a basis for distributing resources or settling claims.

5. *Aggregation.* This refers to the process of reducing the volume of data. A loss of identifiability or information is generally attributed to the process of aggregation, which may be compensated by cost savings in accounting for the information. An optimal level of aggregation is difficult to specify for either financial or management accounting. For financial accounting, the preparation of standard financial statements according to well-defined rules has led to a tendency to aggregate the information at an early stage of information processing. For management

accounting, the lack of homogeneity in the reports, the flexibility in the choice of rules for preparing these reports, and the objective to meet a variety of information needs argue in favor of a management accounting system with less aggregated data, but which takes into account the user's limitations in handling voluminous data.

6. *Flexibility/adaptability.* Flexibility refers to the degree to which data may be the basis for several types of information and reports. It depends on both the classification used for the data base into definite categories and the level of aggregation used in each of the categories. For example, purchases data may be classified under the following categories: (1) by individual product or service, (2) by individual purchaser, (3) by supplier, and so on. These data may be aggregated under the following categories: (1) by transaction, (2) by day, (3) by month, and so on.

Adaptability refers to the extent to which information derived from the data base may be tailored to, or harmonized with, the decision processes of the firm. The adaptability of an accounting system requires not only the presence of flexibility, but also an explicit process of harmonizing it with the decision processes. The committee suggested the following procedures for harmonizing:

> Such harmonizing is often accomplished iteratively through an understanding of the planning and control processes, representing the latter in terms of information parameters and specifying the aggregation rules to be used in going from data base to information and analyzing the impact of such information on the planning and control processes.[20]

Again, given the lack of homogeneity in the management accounting reports, the large number of these reports and the desire to meet various decision needs, management accounting requires higher levels of flexibility and adaptability than financial accounting.

7. *Timeliness.* Timeliness refers to the age of the information. It has two components: interval and delay. Interval is the period of time lapsing between the preparation of two successive reports. Delay is the period of time necessary to process the data, prepare the reports, and distribute them. Timeliness is also related to the concept of *real time.* Boutell provides the following definition:

> It [real time] refers to the time in which information is received by the particular decision maker. If the information is received in sufficient time for a decision to be made without a penalty for delay, the information is said to be received in real time.[21]

Although timeliness is a uniquely desirable property of management accounting information, it is affected by cost considerations and may conflict with other criteria, such as accuracy.

8. *Understandability/acceptability/motivation/fairness.* This refers to the extent to which the user is able to use the information. Understandability refers to the ability of the user to ascertain the message transmitted. Acceptability is the recognition by the user that the problem specification and measurement criteria have been met. Fairness refers to the neutrality of the information as defined earlier. Finally, motivation refers to the attempt to secure goal congruences between the user and the organization. In brief, management accounting information should be understandable, acceptable, fair to the user, and a motivation to the user to perform in the desired manner.

1.4.3 Management accounting concepts

Management accounting concepts based on both the objectives and qualitative characteristics of management accounting would constitute the basic foundation for a management accounting conceptual framework. Although the development and formalization of a management accounting conceptual framework remains to be accomplished, the literature contains references to certain identifiable management accounting concepts. For example, the 1972 AAA Committee on Courses in Managerial Accounting identifies measurement, communication, information, system, planning, feedback, control, and cost behavior as some of the management accounting concepts "which represent a necessary, if not minimum, foundation for the body of knowledge contained within the structure."[22] Accordingly, each of these concepts will be explained next:

1. *Measurement*. Applied to accounting, it has been defined as "an assignment of numerals to an entity's past, present or future economic phenomena, on the basis of past or present observation and according to rules."[23] This concept is very essential to management accounting.

2. *Communication*. As defined by Shannon and Weaver, it encompasses "the procedures by means of which one mechanism affects another mechanism."[24] This concept is also essential in management accounting for allowing the process of moving from measurement to information.

3. *Information*. It represents significant data upon which action is based. It refers to those data that reduce the uncertainty on the part of the user. Thus, data produced by management accounting should be evaluated in terms of their informational content. Although not exhaustive, management accounting information includes the following categories: (1) financial information resulting from the flow of financial resources within the organization, (2) production information resulting from the physical flow of resources within the organization, (3) personnel information resulting from the flow of people within the organization, and (4) marketing information resulting from the interaction with the market for the organization's products.

4. *System*. It refers to an entity consisting of two or more interacting components or subsystems intended to achieve a

goal. Management accounting is generally a subsystem of the accounting information system, which is itself a subsystem of the total management information system within the organization. The interaction of the management accounting system with all the other systems within the organization, and especially the integration of all these systems in complex organizations, is essential for an efficient functioning of the organization. A management accounting system may be defined as *the set of human and capital resources within an organization which is responsible for the production and dissemination of information deemed relevant for internal decision making.*

5. *Planning*. It refers to the management function of setting objectives, establishing policies, and choosing means of accomplishment. Planning may be practiced at different levels in the organization, from strategic to operational, and may have behavioral implications.

6. *Feedback*. It refers to the output of a process which returns to become an input to the process in order to initiate control. It is basically a revision of the planning process to accommodate new environmental events.

7. *Control*. It refers to monitoring and evaluation of performance to determine the degree of conformance of actions to plans. Ideally, planning precedes control, which is followed by a feedback corrective action or a feedforward preventive action.

8. *Cost Behavior*. Cost results from the use of an asset for the generation of revenues. The identification, classification, and estimation of costs is essential to any evaluation of courses of action.

Although not exhaustive, this list represents concepts that are representative of those foundation components essential to a grasp of the management accounting process.

1.4.4 Management accounting techniques

Management accounting techniques should be derived and supported by the management accounting conceptual framework. Given the absence of such a framework, there is no consensus on a list of management accounting techniques. Most management accounting textbooks include standard cost accounting techniques and few attempts at introducing behavioral and/or quantitative considerations in separate chapters. What is needed is a structure that will allow an integration of accounting, organizational, behavioral, quantitative, and other techniques of relevance to internal decision making. The Report of the Committee on Courses in Managerial Accounting proposes such a structure:

- Introductory Material
  - Systems theory and accounting
  - Communications, measurement and information concepts
  - Criteria development
  - Feedback and control mechanisms
  - Information systems
  - Accounting for management planning and control
  - Cost concepts and techniques
- Cost Determination for Assets
  - Job order and process costing
  - Standard costing systems
  - Direct versus absorption costing
  - By-product and joint product costing
  - Cost allocation practices
  - Accounting for human resources
- Planning
  - Strategic planning
  - Continuous planning
  - Investment decisions
  - Comprehensive budgets
  - Cost-volume-profit analysis
  - Problems of alternative choice

Management Control
- Responsibility accounting
- Cost centers
- Financial performance centers
- Investment centers
- Centralized versus decentralized structures
- Concern for goal congruence
- Transfer pricing
- Evaluation methods
- Performance reporting

Operational Control
- Internal control
- Project control
- Inventory control[25]

Although not exhaustive, this list represents most of the techniques included in management accounting textbooks, but still fails to incorporate behavioral, organizational, and decisional models essential to an adequate performance of a management accounting system. Chapters 2 through 4 present most of these nonaccounting considerations that should be incorporated in the body of knowledge known as management accounting.

1.5 CONCLUSIONS

Management accounting has its foundations in the discipline of accounting, although it recognizes the potential benefits of borrowing relevant techniques from other disciplines. It expanded from its limited scope of cost accounting to a multidiscipline integrated field aimed at assisting management in decision making. Although generally perceived as a set of techniques, management accounting includes most of the components of a *conceptual framework*. Such a management accounting conceptual framework is shown in Exhibit 1.1. From a basic objective,

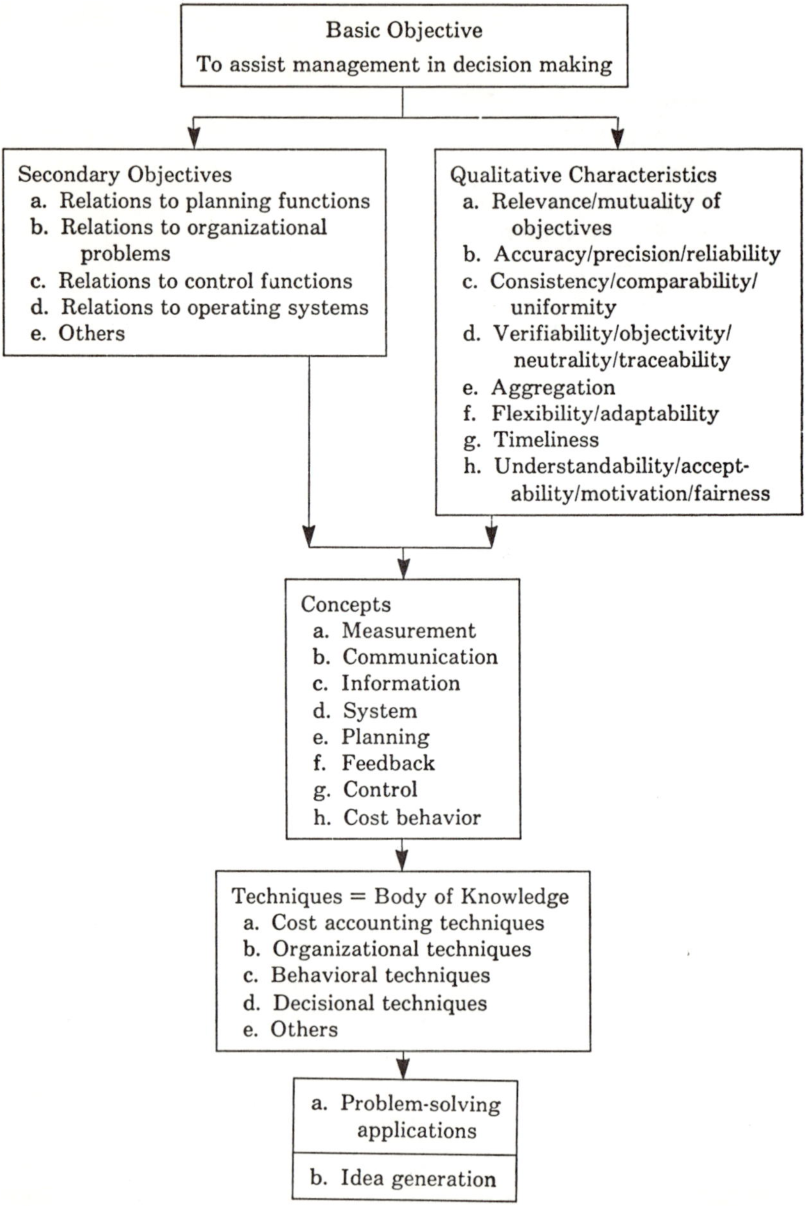

Exhibit 1.1 Tentative management accounting conceptual framework

which is to assist management in decision making, are derived both secondary objectives and qualitative characteristics of management accounting. The management accounting concepts that constitute the foundation components essential to an understanding of the management accounting techniques or body of knowledge rests on their conformance to both the objectives and qualitative characteristics of management accounting. Because of the lack of consensus on these components, the conceptual framework presented in Exhibit 1.1 is only tentative before a formalization by the accounting profession. What must be retained from this exercise is that *management accounting is, first, an accounting subsystem and, second, may be fit in an "emerging" theoretical structure.*

ENDNOTES

1. American Accounting Association (AAA) Committee on Management Accounting, "Report of the 1958 Committee on Management Accounting," *The Accounting Review* (April 1959): 210.
2. William Paton, *Essentials of Accounting* (New York: The Macmillan Company, 1949), p. 2.
3. American Accounting Association, *A Statement of Basic Accounting Theory* (Evanston, Ill.: American Accounting Association, 1966), p. 1.
4. Vergil Boyd and Dale Taylor, "The Magic Words—Managerial Accounting," *The Accounting Review* (January 1961): 111.
5. Harold W. Scott, "Accounting as a Tool of Management," *The Accounting Forum* (May 1958): 30.
6. R. G. Bassett, "Management Accounting Defined," *The Cost Accountant* (October 1962): 386.
7. James S. Earley, "Recent Developments in Cost Accounting and the Marginal Analysis," *The Journal of Political Economy* (June 1955): 299.

8. AAA Committee on Courses in Managerial Accounting, "Report of the Committee on Courses in Managerial Accounting," *The Accounting Review,* Supplement to Vol. 47 (1972): 2.
9. AAA Committee on Management Accounting, "Report of the 1958 Committee on Management Accounting," p. 210.
10. *Webster's Third New International Dictionary* (1971), s.v. *theory.*
11. AAA 1961 Committee on Management Accounting, "Report of the Management Accounting Committee," *The Accounting Review* (July 1962).
12. AAA Committee on Courses in Managerial Accounting, "Report of the Committee on Courses in Managerial Accounting," pp. 6–7.
13. AAA Committee on Managerial Decision Models, "Report of the Committee on Managerial Decision Models," *The Accounting Review,* Supplement to Vol. 44 (1969): 47–58.
14. AAA, *Accounting Theory,* pp. 51–55.
15. AAA Committee on Concepts and Standards—Internal Planning and Control, "Report of the Committee on Concepts and Standards—Internal Planning and Control," *The Accounting Review,* Supplement to Vol. 49 (1974): 83.
16. Ibid., p. 83.
17. AAA, *Accounting Theory,* p. 9.
18. Richard M. Cyert and H. Justin Davidson, *Statistical Sampling for Accounting Information* (Englewood Cliffs, N.J.: Prentice-Hall, Inc., 1962), p. 49.
19. Ibid.
20. AAA Committee on Concepts and Standards—Internal Planning and Control, "Report," p. 91.
21. Wayne S. Boutell, *Computer Oriented Business Systems* (New York: Prentice-Hall, Inc., 1968), p. 152.
22. AAA Committee on Courses in Managerial Accounting, "Report on Courses in Managerial Accounting," p. 7.
23. AAA Committee on Foundations of Accounting Measurement, "Report of the Committee on Foundations of Accounting Measurement," *The Accounting Review,* Supplement to Vol. 46 (1971): 3.

24. Claude E. Shannon and Warren Weaver, *The Mathematical Theory of Communication* (Urbana, Ill.: The University of Illinois Press, 1949), p. 95.
25. AAA Committee on Courses in Managerial Accounting, "Report on Courses in Managerial Accounting," pp. 9–10.

BIBLIOGRAPHY

American Accounting Association, Committee on Courses in Managerial Accounting. "Report of the Committee on Courses in Managerial Accounting." *The Accounting Review,* Supplement to Vol. 47 (1972): 1–14.

______, Committee on Management Accounting. "Report of the 1958 Committee on Management Accounting." *The Accounting Review* (April 1959).

______, Committee on Managerial Decision Models. "Report of the Committee on Managerial Decision Models." *The Accounting Review,* Supplement to Vol. 44 (1969): 43–77.

Boyd, Vergil, and Taylor, Dale. "The Magic Words—Managerial Accounting." *The Accounting Review* (January 1961): 105–111.

Crossman, Paul T. "The Nature of Management Accounting." *The Accounting Review* (April 1958): 222–227.

Davidson, H. Justin, and Trueblood, Robert M. "Accounting for Decision Making." *The Accounting Review* (October 1961): 577–582.

Donbrovski, Willis J. "Managerial Accounting: A Frame of Reference." *Management Accounting* (August 1965).

Firmin, Peter A., and Linn, James J. "Information Systems and Managerial Accounting." *The Accounting Review* (January 1968): 75–82.

Godfrey, James T., and Prince, Thomas R. "The Accounting Model from an Information Systems Perspective." *The Accounting Review* (January 1971): 75–89.

Killough, Larry N. "Does Management Accounting Have a Theoretical Structure?" *Management Accounting* (April 1972).

Kircher, Paul. "Theory and Research in Management Accounting." *The Accounting Review* (January 1961): 43–45.

Shenkin, William G.; Welsh, A.; and Bear, James A., Jr. "Thomas Jefferson: Management Accountant." *The Journal of Accountancy* (April 1972).

Singer, Frank A. "Management Accounting." *The Accounting Review* (January 1961): 112–118.

Chapter Two

THE ORGANIZATIONAL FOUNDATIONS

Management accounting is built on organizational foundations. First, elements of organizational structure shape its techniques, approaches, and role in the firm. Second, it is a function of the theories of organization which describe and explain organizational behavior. Golembiewski was among the first authors to point to the problem of adapting accounting to organization theory and vice versa:

> . . . it seems appropriate that organization theory receive considerable attention by members of the accounting profession, which is presently in the throes of rethinking its scope and methods. For an inappropriate organization structure can frustrate the most worthy of intentions and, in any case, any fundamental changes in accountancy will require changes in the traditional theory of organization.[1]

Thus, management accounting requires a good grasp of the elements of organizational structure and theories of organization. The identification of the elements of an organization structure most prevalent and essential to a proper functioning of a management accounting system allows the tailoring of the internal reporting system to that structure or the suggestion of a more appropriate organization structure. Similarly, the theories of organization point to significant elements that approximate the patterning and order inherent in organizations. Determination of these characteristics guides management accounting to more effective ways of providing its services. Consequently, this chapter will introduce elements of organizational structure and theories of organization most relevant to a proper functioning of management accounting.

2.1 ELEMENTS OF ORGANIZATIONAL STRUCTURE

Formal organizational structure is the aspect of the organization that management often seeks to change in order to improve the functioning of the organization. The elements of this structure affect the ways the management accounting function will be exercised and need to be fully understood by a management accountant. Before presenting these elements of organizational structure most relevant to a proper functioning of management accounting, the nature of an organization will be examined.

2.1.1 Nature of an organization

An organization has been defined as a "relatively permanent and relatively complex discernible interaction system."[2] In other words, the organization is an observable result of the interaction rather than the group of actors. The three components of the definition deserve more clarification.

First, the organization is a *going concern* in the sense that the interaction system is relatively stable. Second, the organization is an *exclusive entity*. It is different from a group or a society in terms of structural complexity. Structural complexity refers to both horizontal and vertical integration. Finally, the organization is an *interaction system*. It assumes the existence of two or more persons who have interdependent relationships. With these in view, three problems appear: (1) organizational membership; (2) organizational boundaries; and (3) organizational environments.

Homans chose to associate organizational membership with the frequency of interaction.[3] If members interact more with each other than with subject *E*, then *E* is not considered a member of the group. To this definition, Hass and Drabeck added two criteria for organizational membership: the frequency of interaction and the content of interaction. In brief, "those interaction units that are perceived high in frequency and similar in content constitute the interaction system."[4]

The organizational boundaries depend on the analyst (for example, the management accountant) and the questions asked by the analyst. Assembling the interaction units in a system on the basis of their frequency and content leads to a delimitation of the boundaries of the organization. The predominant school of thought is that boundaries ought to be viewed as flexible rather than rigid. In recent works of Katz and Kahn[5] and Thompson,[6] organizations are perceived as "open systems."

The functioning of the organization is affected by a multitude of environments. They define the major constraints within which the organization is called to function. The idea is stated well in the following passage from Krupp:

> The range of behavior which the business firm's internal variables will have depends, among other things, on the structure of the market. Under conditions of oligopoly (let us assume the firm is large), phenomena that might appear external and compelling to the small competitive firm become themselves internal and susceptible of manipulation. Thus, the large firm in oligopoly is much more independent of external constraints than is the firm under competition. In a competitive market, on the other hand, the behavior of the firm is largely determined by environmental conditions. The firm in a world of oligopoly is a more self-contained empirical structure than the firm in competition. The independence of the firm from external factors is an empirical matter; empirical structure defines the bounded units of the world of observables.[7]

These environments are characterized by their instability and exclusivity. The nature of an organization as a relatively complex and relatively permanent interaction system places management accounting in the role of an organizational process intended for strengthening these interactions. More specifically, the management accountant will provide essential services that will concretize the interaction between individuals and their membership in the organization, define the boundaries of the organization to include all the interaction units, and structure all analyses, taking into account the constraints imposed by the organizational environments. In brief, interaction units, organizational membership, boundaries, and environment are important organizational concepts that define the scope and the nature of the management accountant's activities.

2.1.2 Organizational structure

Organizational structure is the system of relationships existing among the position holders of an organization. It results from a deliberate and conscious planning of the areas of responsibility, specialization, and authority for each of the organizational members. In general, it takes a hierarchical form where authority and responsibility are differentiated along a vertical dimension, and units, such as departments or divisions, along a horizontal dimension. What results is a pyramidal shaped organization, usually referred to as an organization chart. An example of an organization chart is shown in Exhibit 2.1. Each vertical level in the hierarchy depicts different levels of authority. For example, each of the production centers is responsible to the production superintendent. In turn, the latter, with all the other organizational units on the same horizontal line, is responsible to the manufacturing vice president. Finally, the latter, with all the other vice presidents, is responsible to the manufacturing vice president, who is responsible to the board of directors. Let us note again that each horizontal dimension is differentiated by specialization rather than by authority. This process is termed *departmentalization,* whereby employees are grouped into organizational units on the basis of similar skills and specialization. Growth and environmental change are usually the main determinants for departmentalization. In general, the departmentalization in organizations takes four major forms: by function, by location, by process, and by product. A firm may departmentalize or differentiate horizontally according to one or several of these forms.

First, firms may departmentalize by function. For example, a typical manufacturing firm may include sales, production, ac-

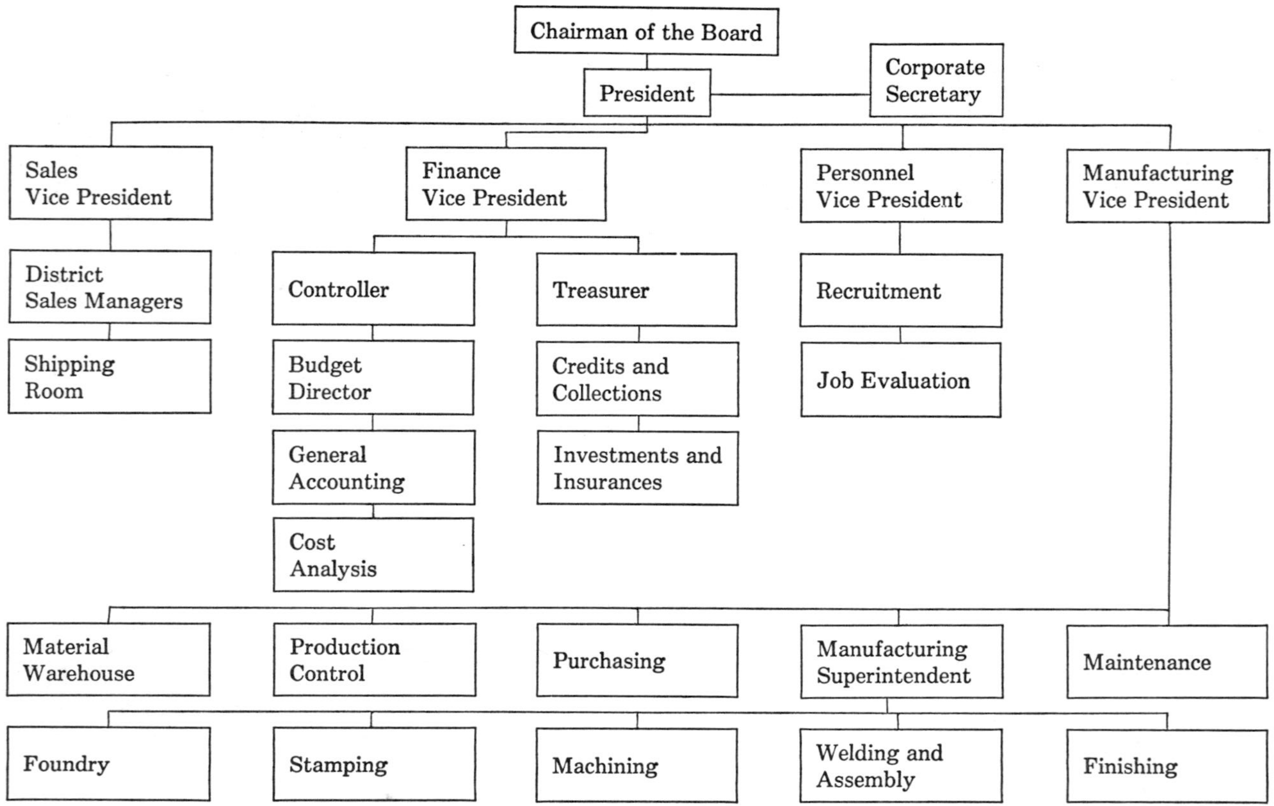

Exhibit 2.1 Organizational chart of a manufacturing company

counting, finance, personnel, research and development, and purchasing as necessary functions to be departmentalized.

Second, firms may departmentalize by process. Most production activities include different technological processes which require different organizational units. In the example presented in Exhibit 2.1, the finishing, foundry, stamping, machining, welding, and assembly are "housed" in different organizational units.

Third, firms may departmentalize by location. A large corporation may be differentiated on the basis of territories, districts, regions, etc. The relatively independent units are referred to as divisions. Hence, a multinational corporation may divisionalize by location to adapt to different legal, taxation, and market environments.

Finally, firms may departmentalize by product. It is beneficial to those firms producing different products for different markets.

Vertical differentiation by authority and responsibility and horizontal differentiation through departmentalization or divisionalization lead to the creation of separate organizational units and necessitate provision for periodic planning and control. This need is only met by the management accounting system in general and responsibility accounting in particular. Management accounting will produce accounting reports of performance and budgets which will serve as the means of communication between these units. Similarly, by making the smallest areas of responsibility the main foundations of the management accounting system, responsibility accounting allows the definition and consolidation of the decisions and the nature of the responsibility of each of the organizational units, and may facilitate effective communication.[8] In brief, while organizational structure is concerned with authority, responsibility, and specialization relations aimed at assuring effective and efficient performance, management accounting, through responsibility accounting, represents the design and implementation of the accounting system for the purpose of better defining and consolidating these relations.

2.1.3 Line and staff relationships

In the organization chart of Exhibit 2.1 the nature of the relationships implied by the lines connecting the organization units boxes has not been explicitly defined. These relationships may be either line or staff. Line implies a basic hierarchical subordinate-superior relationship as defined by the line of authority or chain of command. Line managers are directly responsible for the particular tasks entrusted to them. Staff implies that a part of the managerial task has been assigned by an executive to someone outside the chain of command. Thus, staff managers facilitate the work of the line managers by providing them with essential services. The authority relationships between the staff member and employees of the line at the same or lower levels may be of four types: staff advice, compulsory advice, concurring authority, or limited company authority.[9] Let us examine each type.

1. The "staff advice" is purely advisory. In general, people are inclined to accept the advice of staff managers when they are regarded as technical experts, when they have impressive titles, when they are skilled in presenting ideas, when they have potential backing by a senior operating executive, and when their views may influence the reward and penalty system. In short, "even though a staff man may have no command authority whatsoever, he may still get his recommendations accepted if he is smart, persuasive, impressive, and influential."[10]

2. Staff managers may have a "compulsory advice" relationship in the sense that they must always be consulted before action is taken.

3. Staff managers may have a "concurring authority" relationship in the sense that no action can be taken until a designated staff manager agrees to it.

4. Finally, staff managers may have a "functional authority" or "limited company authority" relationship in the sense that they are authorized to personally give direct orders to operating personnel rather than merely making recommendations to line managers. For example, the financial accounting department may decide that certain production statistics ought to be disclosed in the annual reports, forcing the production department to produce them periodically.

The concepts of line and staff are another element of organizational structure of relevance to management accounting. First, management accounting is a process that provides services and assistance to other units in the organization. Its role is supportive by nature. It is basically a staff function. Second, as a staff manager the management accountant's authority may range from purely advisory to limited company authority. Third, because of the great need for the specialized knowledge provided by the management accounting department, it is likely to be positioned rather highly in the organization. In any case, management accounting is a decision support system.

2.1.4 The controllers in the organization

The managers in charge of accounting departments are known as controllers. They are staff members of the top management team and are line managers in their own departments. As a member of the staff, they advise management in the areas of corporate reporting, planning, and control. Controllers' activities include mainly the following:

1. They are responsible for the supervision of all the facets of financial accounting leading to the publication of annual reports.

2. They coordinate all the activities leading to the establishment of the master budget and long-term plan of the firm.
3. They promote through proper circulation of performance reports the maintenance of a system of control.
4. As designers and activators of the basic organizational communication system, the electronic data processing system, controllers act as the essential persons for a proper collection, diffusion, and channeling of relevant and timely information.

The role of controllers varies, however, from one firm to another, covering the total continuum of staff work. In other words, their role may be a purely advisory relationship, a "compulsory advice" relationship, a "concurring authority" relationship, or an effective "functional authority" relationship.

Because of their position in the top management team, controllers are overseers of the work of others. They initiate and direct the preparation of specific reports for internal or external reporting, and they advise top management on key issues.

Generally reporting to controllers are the staff department of electronic data processing, taxes, financial analysis and budgeting, financial services, corporate accounting, management services, and payroll. It shows that corporate controllers have moved to the important and central stage. Consider the following quotation:

> As the controller's job has changed so have the tools of the trade. In the old days, the controller simply worked up the profit and loss statement and the balance sheet. Today the job involves elaborate monitoring and cross checking of scads of financial data from profits and expenses to return on investment and the cost of capital. Instead of the adding machine and ledger books, the controller works with increasingly complex, sophisticated computer programs that keep him in almost daily touch with almost every facet of the business.[11]

The increase in the size and complexity of business entities, the growth in the use of the planning and control technique, and the new enlarged scope of management accounting activities are the reasons for this new controller concept. It is a top level function with a primary responsibility for the detailed analysis and interpretation of operating results, policies, procedures, and proposals of major importance. The job of controllers is then difficult to define and depends on the particular organizational structure of the firm and the role and scope of the accounting activities. In any case, the job is a complex one. The large list of activities implies that controllers must have personal, educational, and experience qualifications in order to handle all these duties properly. These requirements are very important, given the new expanded role of management accounting in the organization as the "director of management information." Controllers are also essential to the acceptance of the new nature and uses of management accounting. Some of their tasks may involve teaching and convincing the rest of the organization about the new scope of management accounting.

2.2 THEORIES OF ORGANIZATION

The theories of organization represent different attempts in the literature to describe and explain organizational behavior. Each of these theories attempts to determine the significant elements that may approximate the patterning or order existing in organizations. Because these elements comprise the key organizational variables or the ways they are related, they define the ways management accounting will better provide its services to the organization. Although not exhaustive, the theories examined comprise those that currently reflect organizational literature, namely: (1) the rational perspective, (2) the classical perspective, (3) the human relations perspective, and (4) the natural system perspective. Management accounting is thought to rest on elements provided by each of these formulations, rather than on any single one, because none provides an entirely adequate theory of organization on its own.

2.2.1 The rational perspective

Weber argued that the social behavior and the social interaction of individuals depend on their "ideas" of the existence of a *legitimate authority.*[12] He distinguished between three pure types of legitimate authority, each dependent on a different source of legitimation. They are the following:

1. *Traditional authority,* legitimated by time and resting "on an established belief in the sanctity of immemorial traditions and the legitimacy of the status of those exercising authority under them."[13]
2. *Charismatic authority,* legitimated by the appealing personality of the leader and resting on the "devotion to the specific and exceptional sanctity, heroism or exemplary character of an individual person, and of the normative patterns or order revealed or ordained by him."[14]
3. *Bureaucratic or rational-legal authority,* legitimated by rules and resting "on a belief in the 'legality' of patterns of normative rules and the right of those elevated to authority under such rules to issue commands."[15]

The last type of authority was viewed by Weber as an ideal characteristic of modern organizations. He drew attention to the fact that in modern society the bureaucratic type has become dominant because of its alleged greater efficiency. The bureaucratic organization is composed of a bureaucratic administrative staff. The position occupied by the chief of such an organization is by virtue of appropriation, election, or succession. The individuals comprising the organization conform to the following ten criteria:

1. They are personally free and subject to authority only with respect to their impersonal official obligations.
2. They are organized in a clearly defined hierarchy of offices.
3. Each office has a clearly defined sphere of competence in the legal sense.
4. The office is filled by a free contractual relationship. Thus, in principle, there is free selection.
5. Candidates are selected on the basis of technical qualifications. In the most rational case, this is tested by examination or guaranteed by diplomas certifying technical training, or both. They are appointed, not elected.
6. They are remunerated by fixed salaries in money, for the most part with a right to pensions. Only under certain circumstances does the employing authority, especially in private organizations, have a right to terminate the appointment, but the official is always free to resign. The salary scale is primarily graded according to rank in the hierarchy; but in addition to this criterion, the responsibility of the position and the requirements of the incumbent's social status may be taken into account.
7. The office is treated as the sole, or at least the primary, occupation of the incumbent.
8. It constitutes a career. There is a system of promotion according to seniority or achievement, or both. Promotion is dependent on the judgment of superiors.
9. The official works entirely separated from ownership of the means of administration and without appropriation of his position.
10. He is subject to strict and systematic discipline and control in the conduct of his office.[16]

The organization under a rational perspective is viewed as a highly efficient machine where a group of members strive together in an orderly fashion to complete a given objective. Empirical evidence related to the organizational effectiveness of the Weberian type of organization was provided by Price.[17]

Different points of criticism appear in the literature against the rational perspective in organizational structure and behavior. Organizations tend to change from bureaucratic to charismatic during crisis situations. Weber uniquely assumed a formal behavior existing in the organization. People within the organization were assumed to behave rigidly and mechanistically according to established rules. Thus, informal behavior, group norms, environmental changes, and internal conflict are not discussed by Weber, who provided the first of the original studies designed to examine the nature and functioning of bureaucracy and organizations in general.

Despite its apparent limitations, the rational perspective designates significant elements approximating the patterning or order inherent in organizations and of relevance to management accounting. Organizations may be seen as a deliberate, rational arrangement of means to accomplish a desired end. Rules are established in order to regulate the organization's structure and processes. Finally, legal authority is used to coordinate all the elements of an organization in order to allow their efficient functioning. In response to these patterns, management accounting will focus on the legally prescribed structures and the mechanisms by which they are maintained. For example, control will focus on whether persons comply with organizational rules given that each person's actions are essential to the accomplishment of the organizational goals. Similarly, management accounting as a form of organizational behavior will be consciously and rationally administered with the organizational goals in mind.

2.2.2 The classical perspective

The classical school originated with Taylor and his "Principles of Scientific Management."[18] The concern was with insuring the most efficient utilization of the physical resources of the organization. Scientific management was based on four main principles:

1. The development of an ideal or best method primarily through time and motion study.
2. The selection and development of workers.
3. The combination between the best method and the best selected and trained workers.
4. The close cooperation of managers and workers.

Taylor's approach led to major advances in industrial efficiency and influenced the works of Gantt[19] and Gilbreth.[20]

The main goal of scientific management is to use scientific methods to establish a standard for completing a job in the best manner. The productive processes are concerned with the ratio of output to input, *the criterion of efficiency*. To accomplish these objectives, the work force is to be organized so that each person is assigned a standard for his or her highly specialized job, based on the most efficient method of completing the work and rewarded on the basis of task accomplishment. From these objectives stem two basic characteristics of the organization. It is *work centered* and *authoritarian*. The central characteristic of an organization is work and, given that work is considered distasteful by some, authority is necessary for insuring the accomplishment of organizational objectives. Authority is centralized and flows from the owners to the board of directors to the workers. The authority of the president lies in POSDCORB.[21] The acronym stands for Planning, Organizing, Staffing, Directing, Coordinating, Reporting, and Budgeting. Work is specialized in units, leading to what is known as the departmentalized approach to the problem of management. These units are coordinated in a hierarchical structure. The authority in each unit is defined by the "span of control" of each manager. All these characteristics reflect a facet of the traditional school known as "the principles of management" or "administrative management theory." Fayol, in particular, viewed the principles of management as follows:

1. Division of work
2. Authority
3. Discipline
4. Unity of command
5. Unity of direction
6. Subordination of individual interests to the general interest
7. Remuneration
8. Centralization
9. Scalar chain (line of authority)
10. Order
11. Equity
12. Stability of tenure of personnel
13. Initiative
14. Esprit de corps.[22]

The classical school has also had its share of criticisms. It has been labeled as normative rather than analytical. Like the Weberian model, it has ignored the impact of the external environment, the existence of internal conflict, and the behavioral idiosyncrasies resulting from the different cognitive make-up of organization members.

Like the Weberian perspective, the classical perspective identifies elements approximating the patterning or order inherent in organizations and of relevance to management accounting. Organizations are viewed only as means in the pursuit of a specific end, defined as optimal organizational efficiency. The accomplishment of this objective lies in the arrangement of the employees and machines. This arrangement relies on scientific means of associating the best person and/or machine to the ideal job. It requires developing scientific standards rather than rules of thumb for each individual and each task.

> The work of every workman is fully planned out by the management at least one day in advance, and each man received in most cases complete written instructions, describing in detail the task which he is to accomplish, as well as the means to be used in doing the work.[23]

Briefly, the classical perspective rests on management accounting by calling for both planning and control: Planning by the setting of rigid scientific standards for each job, and control by insuring the realization of *optimal organizational efficiency.* Let us note, however, that the classical perspective calls for planning and control primarily at the operative or worker level, and essentially short range and specific. What may then be learned and extrapolated from the classical perspective is the requirement of planning and control at all levels of management, short term and long term, towards the realization of the optimal organizational efficiency.

2.2.3 The human relations perspective

As a counterpoint against the impersonality of classical theory, the human relations perspective emphasizes the human dimension of management. The major thrust of this perspective is that:

> The dominant focus of organization was transformed from a rational model, free from the friction of man's emotions, to a model which appears to be less determined and unfathomable. That is, the new look in organizational theory took cognizance of the unanticipated consequences of organizations: workers' feelings, beliefs, perceptions, ideas, and sentiments—exactly those elements of passion Weber believed escaped calculation. Administrators began to take seriously—in part through the seminal work of several social scientists—not only their formal organiza-

> tional chart, but workers' feelings about the structure and hierarchy. This model of organization . . . took as its major assumption that man could be motivated to work more productively on the basis of fulfilling certain psychological needs. This "new look" of organization was no less rational than the earlier machine model, except that man's motivation was a tricker and more elusive concept than the machine.[24]

This perspective started when Elton May and other Harvard University professors were invited to study new ways to increase plant productivity at the Hawthorne plant of the Western Electric Company. Known as the Hawthorne Studies, they showed that workers are complex social creatures with feelings, desires, and fears, and they react to change in terms of the meaning change has for them. What change meant to workers depended on their *social conditioning* (feelings, fears, hope, etc.) and their *social situation* at work where group pressures determined attitudes and sentiments. Other similar findings were included in *Management and the Worker,* the publication resulting from the Hawthorne experiment.[25] This line of research was pursued through the empirical works of such theorists as Rensis Likert,[26] Chris Argyris, [27] and Douglas McGregor.[28]

What stems from the human relations perspective is that workers are social creatures with feelings, desires, and fears, and they are motivated by attitudes formed through interactions in the formal group rather than uniquely by economic factors. Group norms act as a major regulatory tool, affecting member behavior given that persons desire group acceptance. Thus, the organizations become essentially sets of interlocked functioning groups. Likert suggests that these groups may be linked together to create a working organization where each individual will increase a sense of participation because each individual is more aware of the congruence between personal goals and the company's objectives.[29] In fact, Likert advocated the use of the participative group type of management system as the most effective, rather than the exploitive-authoritative, benevolent-authoritative, and consultative systems.[30] These characteristics of the human relations perspectives have great implications for management accounting. First, management accounting concepts and techniques, in general, and planning and control, in particular, have to take into account the individuals and what motivates them. "Each of us wants appreciation, recognition, influence, a feeling of accomplishment, and a feeling that people who are important to us believe in us and respect us."[31] Second, it implies that workers should be involved in some participatory ways in the setting of standards. Preferably group norms should be considered in the setting of standards with an emphasis on cooperation rather than competition among group members.

> The best performance, lower costs, and the highest level of earnings and of employee satisfaction occur when the drive for a sense of personal worth is used to create strong motivational forces to *cooperate* rather than *compete* with one's peers and colleagues. The use of this motive in ways which yield cooperative rather than competitive relationships appears to yield stronger motivational forces oriented toward achieving the organization's objectives and is accompanied by positive rather than negative side effects. Subordinates aid each other and share leadership tasks rather than putting immediate self-interest ahead of long-range self-interest and organizational success.[32]

Third, performance reports used for control should not be limited to financial data and should be expanded to include a measure of the "organizational atmosphere" or climate which determines workers' productivity.

2.2.4 The natural system perspective

The natural system perspective views organizations as continually adapting to a changing environment in order to maintain equilibrium. Once created, the organizations acquire a life of their own and behave in unplanned and spontaneous or "natural" ways. This perspective is best illustrated in the works of three sociologists: Michels,[33] Parsons,[34] and Selznick.[35] For example, Selznick emphasizes "cooptation" as a predominant adaptive process of organization; that is, "the process of absorbing new elements in the leadership or policy-determining structure of an organization as one means of averting threats to its stability or existence."[36] These continuous attempts at adapting to their environments lead the organizations to modify their basic structures and create a character or personality. The structure of an organization, therefore, is inseparable from the functioning of the organization.[37]

Viewed as a system, the organization stresses the interdependence of parts or subsystems. These are: (1) the productive subsystem responsible for the technical processes, (2) the supportive subsystems responsible for the efficient flow of inputs in the organization and output out of the organization, (3) the maintenance subsystem responsible for the maintenance of the organization by recruiting and rewarding the members, (4) the adaptive subsystem responsible for responding to the environmental changes, and (5) the managerial subsystem responsible for directing and controlling all other subsystems.

The natural system perspective, like the other perspectives, identifies elements and characteristics of importance to management accounting. First, each organization acquires a given personality which will require specific management techniques different from those adopted by other organizations. "Every structure has a set of basic needs and develops systematic means of self-defense."[38] Second, because the organization faces a given changing environment, it must change and adapt to the new environmental conditions requiring management accounting to be dynamic in the sense of continuously absorbing new elements and information into its reporting function, adapting old techniques, and adopting new techniques to avert threats to the stability or existence of the organization. Third, the control process should rely on feedforward techniques which precipitate internal changes. Fourth, because the organization is a collec-

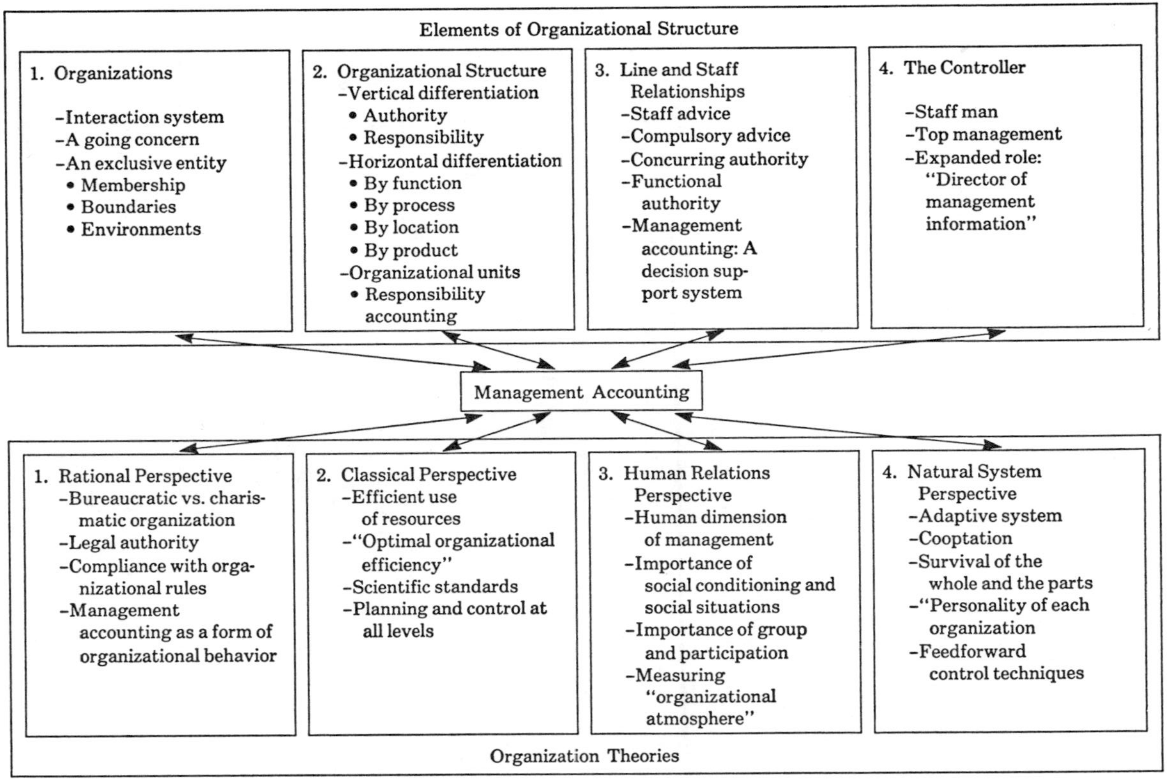

Exhibit 2.2 Management accounting: The organizational foundations

tion of subsystems, each trying to maintain its own equilibrium, management accounting should be designed to serve the subsystems and to maintain their autonomy. Deliberate changes can be made without affecting other subsystems because each subsystem is part of an organic whole.

2.3 CONCLUSIONS

Management accounting rests on organizational foundations. The elements of organizational structure and the theories of organization define its role and scope in the organization and the techniques, approaches, and philosophies it may espouse in order to provide adequate services to the organization. From the elements of organizational structure, the nature of organizations, the nature of organizational structure, the implications of the line/staff relationships, and the new role of controllers provide management accounting with different organizational concepts which define and shape some of its techniques and approaches. From the organization theories, the rational perspective, the classical perspective, the human relations perspective, and the natural system perspective point to significant elements which approximate the patterning and order inherent in organizations, and which may direct management accounting to more effective ways of providing its services. These relationships between management accounting and the elements of organization structure and organization theories are illustrated in Exhibit 2.2.

ENDNOTES

1. Robert T. Golembiewski, "Accountancy as a Function of Organizational Theory," *The Accounting Review* (April 1964): 341.
2. Eugene J. Hass and Thomas E. Drabeck, *Complex Large Organizations: A Sociological Perspective* (New York: The Macmillan Publishing Co., Inc., 1973), p. 8.

3. George Homans, *The Human Group* (New York: Harcourt, Brace and Jovanovich, Inc., 1950), pp. 82–86.
4. Hass and Drabeck, *Complex Large Organizations,* p. 14.
5. Donald Katz and Robert L. Kahn, *The Social Psychology of Organizations* (New York: John Wiley & Sons, Inc., 1966), p. 172.
6. James D. Thompson, *Organizations in Action* (New York: McGraw-Hill Book Co., 1967).
7. Sherman Krupp, *Pattern in Organizational Analysis* (New York: Holt, Rinehart & Winston, Inc., 1961), p. 60.
8. George J. Benston, "The Role of the Firm's Accounting System for Motivation," *The Accounting Review* (April 1963): p. 348.
9. Don Hellriegel and John W. Slocum, Jr., *Management: A Contingency Approach,* 2nd ed. (Reading, Mass.: Addison-Wesley, 1979).
10. William H. Newman, Charles E. Summer, and Warren E. Kirby, *The Process of Management—Concepts, Behavior and Practice,* 2nd ed. (Englewood Cliffs, N.J.: Prentice-Hall, Inc., 1962), p. 110.
11. "The Controller: Inflation Gives More Power with Management," *Business Week* (August 5, 1977): 85.
12. Max Weber, *Basic Concepts in Sociology,* trans. H. P. Secher (New York: The Citadel Press, 1962).
13. Max Weber, *The Theory of Social and Economic Organization,* trans. Alexander M. Henderson and Talcott Parsons (New York: The Free Press, 1947), p. 328.
14. Ibid.
15. Ibid.
16. Ibid., pp. 404–405.
17. James L. Price, *Organizational Effectiveness: An Inventory of Propositions* (Homewood, Ill.: Richard D. Irwin, Inc., 1968).
18. Frederick W. Taylor, *Scientific Management* (New York: Harper and Row, 1947).
19. Henry L. Gantt, *Work Wages and Profits* (Easton, Pa.: Hive, 1973).
20. Frank B. Gilbreth, *Bricklaying System* (Easton, Pa.: Hive, 1972); see also *Motion Study* (Easton, Pa.: Hive, 1972).

21. Luther Gulick, "Notes on the Theory of Organizations," *Papers on the Science of Administration,* eds. Luther Gulick and Lyndall F. Urwick (New York: Institute of Public Administration, Columbia University, 1937).
22. H. Fayol, *General Principles of Management* (New York: Pitman, 1949), Chapter 4, p. 19.
23. Taylor, *Scientific Management,* p. 40.
24. W. G. Bennis, "Some Problems in Organization and Administration," *Hospital Administration* (1959).
25. Fritz J. Roethlisberger and William J. Dickson, *Management and the Worker* (Cambridge, Mass.: Harvard University Press, 1939).
26. Rensis Likert, *New Patterns of Management* (New York: McGraw-Hill Book Co., 1961).
27. Chris Argyris, *Integrating the Individual and the Organization* (New York: John Wiley and Sons, Inc., 1964); and *Understanding Organizational Behavior* (Homewood, Ill.: The Dorsey Press, Inc., 1960).
28. Douglas McGregor, *The Human Side of Enterprise* (New York: McGraw-Hill Book Co., 1960); and *The Professional Manager,* Caroline McGregor and Warren G. Bennis, eds. (New York: McGraw-Hill Book Co., 1967).
29. Likert, *New Patterns of Management,* p. 240.
30. Ibid., pp. 223–33.
31. Ibid., p. 98.
32. Rensis Likert, *The Human Organization* (New York: McGraw-Hill Book Co., 1967), p. 75.
33. Robert Michels, *Political Parties,* trans. Eden Paul and Cedar Paul (New York: The Free Press, 1949), first published 1915.
34. Talcott Parsons, *The Social System* (New York: The Free Press, 1951); Talcott Parsons, "Suggestions for a Sociological Approach to Theory of Organizations," *Administrative Science Quarterly* (June 1956): 63–85.
35. Philip Selznick, *TVA and the Grass Roots* (Berkeley and Los Angeles: University of California Press, 1949).
36. Ibid., p. 13.
37. Daniel Katz and Robert L. Kahn, *The Social Psychology of Organizations* (New York: Wiley, 1966).
38. Selznick, *TVA and the Grass Roots* p. 252.

BIBLIOGRAPHY

Benston, George J. "The Role of the Firm's Accounting System for Motivation." *The Accounting Review* (April 1963): 347–54.

Golembiewski, Robert T. "Organization Theory and the New Accountancy: One Avenue of Revolution." *Quarterly Review of Economics and Business* (Summer 1963): 29–40.

______. "Accountancy as a Function of Organizational Theory." *Accounting Theory* (April 1964): 333–41.

Gordon, M. J. "Toward a Theory of Responsibility Accounting Systems." *N.A.A. Bulletin* (December 1963): 3–9.

Gulick, Luther, and Urwick, Lyndall F., eds. *Papers on the Science of Administration* (New York: Institute of Public Administration, Columbia University, 1937).

Hass, Eugene, and Drabeck, Thomas E. *Complex Large Organizations: A Sociological Perspective* (New York: MacMillan Publishing Co., Inc., 1973).

Katz, Daniel, and Kahn, Robert C. *The Social Psychology of Organizations* (New York: Wiley, 1966).

Price, James L. *Organizational Effectiveness: An Inventory of Propositions* (Homewood, Ill.: Richard D. Irwin, Inc., 1968).

Roethlisberger, Fritz J., and Dickson, William J. *Management and the Worker* (Cambridge, Mass.: Harvard University Press, 1939).

Simon, H. A.; Guetzkow, H.; Kozmetsky, G.; and Tyndall, G. *Centralization Versus Decentralization in Organizing the Controller's Department* (New York: Controllership Foundation, Inc.).

Chapter Three

THE BEHAVIORAL FOUNDATIONS

Management accounting is built on behavioral foundations. Its explicit aim is to affect the behavior of individuals in a desirable direction. To accomplish this purpose, management accounting has to be adapted to the different characteristics which shape the "cognitive make-up" of individuals within an organization and affect their performance. In general, these characteristics pertain to three factors: (1) the perception by the individual of what should be the objective function or goals in the firm; (2) the various factors likely to motivate the individual to perform; and (3) the decision-making model most relevant to particular contexts and most preferred by the individual. Although these factors do not constitute an exhaustive list of the behavioral concepts likely to affect the performance of an individual within an organization, they have been identified in the literature of various disciplines as essential factors to be considered for an understanding of an individual behavior within an organization and the design of any information system.

Thus, management accounting requires a good grasp of the behavioral concepts; namely, the objective function in management accounting, motivation theories, and models of decision making. Each of these concepts identifies factors and situations which influence the individual behavior and indicates avenues for management accounting to adapt its services.

3.1 THE OBJECTIVE FUNCTION IN MANAGEMENT ACCOUNTING

Many authors in the field of complex organizations define an organization as a social system that is created to achieve certain specific goals or objectives. For example, Etzioni defines organizations as "social units (or human groupings) deliberately constructed and reconstructed to seek specific goals."[1] Hall states:

> An organization is a collectivity with a relatively identifiable boundary, a normative order, authority ranks, community systems, and membership coordinating systems; this collectivity

> exists on a relatively continuous basis in an environment and engages in activities that are usually related to a goal or a set of goals.[2]

The concept of organizational goal and/or objective has not, however, been clearly defined in the literature. The general goals refer to the intentions or wishes espoused by those persons who develop them. For example, Buck gives the following operational definition of organizational goals:

> It is the decision to commit resources for certain activities and to withhold them from certain others that operationally defines the organization's goals. Verbal pronouncements are insufficient for defining goals; the speaker must put his resources where his mouth is if something is to be considered a goal.[3]

Different typologies of goals have also been proposed. First, Thompson differentiated between goals held *for* an organization and goals *of* an organization.[4] The former are held by persons who are not members of the organization but have a given interest in the activities of the firm, such as clientele, investors, action groups, etc. The latter are held by persons who are part of the "dominant coalition" in terms of holding enough control to commit the organization to a given direction.

Perrow made a distinction between "official goals" and "operative goals."[5] Official goals refer to those objectives or general purposes stated either orally or in writing by key members. Operative goals refer to the designated objectives based on the actual operating policies of the organization. Etzioni refers to such goals as real goals. They constitute:

> The future states toward which a majority of the organizational means and major organizational commitments . . . are directed, and which, in cases of conflict with goals which are stated but command few resources, have clear priority.[6]

Each discipline conceives a different goal or objective in its examination of profit-oriented organizations. The discipline of economics, for example, in its neoclassical approach views profit maximization as the single determinant of behavior. As seen in Chapter 2, organizational and management theories have provided various behavioral theories of the firm. In management accounting, as in corporate finance, neither the economic model nor the behavioral model appears entirely suitable. In fact, both models have influenced three held views of business behavior applicable to management accounting: the shareholder wealth maximization model, the managerial welfare maximization model, and the social welfare maximization model.[7] Each of these models constitutes an acceptable objective of profit-oriented organizations in the field of management accounting. Because the scope and practice of management accounting is heavily influenced by these assumptions, each of them will be examined next.

3.1.1 The stockholder wealth maximization model

In most textbooks in the field of corporate finance and specifically in management accounting, authors operate on the assumption that management's primary goal is to maximize the wealth of its stockholders. This view is referred to as the shareholder wealth maximization (SWM) model. According to SWM model, the firm accepts all projects yielding more than the cost of capital, and in equity financing prefers retaining earnings to issuing new stocks. It also assumes that earnings are objectively determined to show the true financial position of the firm to its owners and other users. In fact, the SWM model translates into maximizing the price of the common stock. Management is assumed to use decision rules and techniques which are in the best interests of the stockholders. In a management accounting context, SWM implies an acceptance by management of budgeting and control standards, a rejection of slack budgeting, any suboptimizing behavior, and an adoption of management accounting techniques that are in the best interests of the owners of the firm. If management behaves otherwise, its right to manage may be either questioned or revoked, given that stockholders own the firm and elect the management team. Solomon made a similar suggestion as follows:

> But what if management has other motives, such as maximizing sales or size, growth or market share, or their own survival, or peace of mind? These operating goals do not necessarily conflict with the operating goal of wealth maximization. Indeed, a good case could be made for the thesis that wealth maximization also maximizes the achievement of these other objectives. But the point of issue is what if there is a conflict? What, for example, if management's quest for its own peace of mind or for some other goal consistently leads it to reject operating decisions that should be accepted by the wealth-maximizing criterion? The traditional answer is that such a management will be replaced sooner or later, and this is the only answer possible. Legally, management governs only as the appointed representatives of the owners. It may reject over-all goals which promote the exclusive interest of owners so long as it substitutes goals which are designed to promote that of society as a whole. But if it rejects owner-oriented goals and socially-oriented goals in favor of goals that are solely management-oriented and which lead to substantially different courses of action, its right to govern is open to question.[8]

3.1.2 The managerial welfare maximization model

Another school of thought maintains that a different objective function other than shareholder wealth maximization exists for the firm, namely, that managers run firms for their own benefits. It is maintained that because the stock of most large firms is widely held, the managers of such firms have a great deal of freedom. This being the case, they may be tempted for personal benefits to pursue an objective other than shareholder welfare maximization. This school of thought is generally referred to as the managerial welfare maximization (MWM) model. So rather than maximizing profits, the managers may maximize sales or assets,[9] the rate of growth,[10] or managerial utility.[11] As a consequence, managers may engage in suboptimization schemes as long as they contribute to their own welfare. For example, an entrenched management may avoid risky ventures even though the returns to stockholders were high enough to justify the endeavor. In a management accounting context, MWM implies a lesser acceptance by management of budgeting and control standards, a recourse to slack budgeting and any suboptimization behavior, a manipulation or avoidance within legality of full disclosure in order to present the firm's operation favorably, i.e., income smoothing, and finally, adoption of management accounting techniques that are in the best interest of managers. In a recent survey, Branch concludes as follows:

> The evidence to date may be summarized as follows. Many managers have considerable discretion to substitute their own interests for that of the stockholders. Stockholder and manager interests can conflict or be independent in significant respects. The extent to which firms are managed in stockholder interests vary considerably. Most of the empirical work suggests that firms managed in stockholders' interests tend in some sense to outperform management-oriented firms.[12]

That managers may elect to substitute their own different interests raises the question of how goals within MWM are "determined" or "set" in decisions to commit the organization to a particular course of action. Three distinct models have been identified to represent the goal-setting processes.[13] These are the bargaining model, the problem-solving model, and the coalition model. Because they present good conceptualizations of the goal determination process under MWM, they are briefly presented next.[14]

The bargaining model. The bargaining model depicts goal determination as the result of an open-ended negotiation process among all interested parties leading to a series of trade-offs and compromises. It is based on three important assumptions:

1. There is an active group of participants (internal or external) who impose demands on the organization.

2. These demands are conflicting. They cannot be accommodated simultaneously.
3. The individuals or groups are interdependent.[15]

The problem-solving model. The problem-solving model describes goal determination as the result of successive decisions made by high level administrators. It is based on three important assumptions:

1. Policy commitments are made within a set of constraints or requirements that are known to decision makers.
2. These constraints can be ranked and a preferred set accommodated.
3. The goals of different individuals or groups can be simultaneously satisfied.[16]

The dominant coalition model. Given the existence of controlling interests in the firm, the dominant coalition model describes goal determination as the result of decisions made by those who control the ends to which policies and resources are committed. It is based on two assumptions:

1. There are many persons or groups who hold goals for an organization. These goals are frequently in conflict and cannot all be accommodated.
2. One individual or group does not have sufficient power alone to act unilaterally. Power is dispersed. Collective behavior is required to secure support for goals.[17]

3.1.3 The social welfare maximization model

The climate in which businesses operate is changing with pressures on organizations to be more sensitive to the impact of behavior on society. In adopting a more socially responsible attitude and responding to the pressures of new dimensions—social, human, and environmental—organizations may have to alter their main objective, whether SWM or MWM, to include as an additional constraint the welfare of society at large. This view may be referred to as the social welfare maximization (SOWM) model. Under SOWM, the firm undertakes all projects which, in addition to the usual profitability objective, minimize the social costs and maximize social benefits created by the productive operations of the firm. Thus, under SOWM the firm is not only liable to the shareholders and managers, but also to the society at large. Given the different interest groups in the society at large, the organization may have to develop different corporate purposes. For example, it was reported that one corporate group has defined eight corporate purposes: "profit, sensitivity to natural and human environment, growth, responsiveness to consumer needs, equitable distributions of benefits, dynamic business structure, fair treatment of employees, and legal and ethical behavior."[18]

In a management accounting context, SOWM implies the developing of a social reporting system oriented toward the measurement of social performance, including not only social costs, but social benefits. It suggests the development of a new concept of organization performance which will be more indicative of the firm's social responsibility than is provided by conventional accounting. For example, the AAA Committee on Measurement of Social Cost suggested a total organization performance which is a function of "five outputs":

1. Net income, which benefits stockholders and provides resources for further business growth.
2. Human resource contribution, which assists the individual in the organization to develop new knowledge or skills.
3. Public contribution, which helps the organization's community to function and provides services for its constituency.
4. Environmental contribution (closely allied with public contribution), which affects "quality of life" for society.
5. Product or service contribution, which affects customer well-being and satisfaction.[19]

However, regardless of the objective function adopted by managers, social reporting, and particularly social reports, are needed by management for relevant decision making and to comply with both social pressures and legal requirements.

3.2 MOTIVATION THEORIES

Motivation is related to the intrinsic forces within the individual; namely, the motives and unsatisfied needs of the individual. More explicitly, it is concerned with "how behavior gets started, is energized, is sustained, is directed, is stopped, and what kind of subjective reaction is presented in the organization while all this is going on."[20] For this reason, motivation is important for an organization and for management accounting. It basically refers to an individual's needs or motives that make that individual act in a specific manner. It relates all aspects of individual behavior where a deliberate and conscious action is initiated in the organization to direct individuals so that they can satisfy their needs as much as possible while they strive to accomplish the objectives of the organization. These actions may be either initiated directly by the managers' actions or through the adoption of appropriate management accounting techniques. Thus, management accounting techniques necessitate a good grasp of motivation in organizations. The identification of the factors and situations that may influence and coordinate employee action allows the management accountant to adapt the services to offer to the realities of human behavior. The literature on motivation identifies five theories of motivation: the need theory, the two-factor theory, the value/expectancy theory, the achievement theory, and the inequity theory. Each of these theories either identifies what factors within the individual and his or her environment activate high performance, or attempts to explain and describe the process of how behavior is activated, what directs it, and how it is controlled and stopped. Let us examine each of these theories of motivation and their implications for management accounting.

3.2.1 Need theory

Originally advanced by Abraham Maslow, need theory holds that people are motivated to satisfy a "hierarchy" of needs.[21] These needs are as follows (in ascending order of prepotency):

1. *The physiological needs:* food, shelter, warmth, and other bodily wants.
2. *The safety needs:* security and protection.
3. *The need for love and belongingness:* desire to both give and receive love and friendship.
4. *The need for esteem:* self-respect and the respect of others.
5. *The self-actualization need:* "What a man *can* be, he *must* be."

Thus, individuals strive to satisfy these needs in a sequential fashion, starting with the physiological needs. The process of deprivation-domination-gratification-activation continues until the self-actualization need has been activated. This suggests that once the basic physiological needs and safety needs are satisfied, individuals will respond better to rewards leading to self-respect and self-actualization than to economic rewards which are primarily related to the satisfaction of lower-level needs. What this implies for management accounting is that assuming individuals in the organization are well paid, the emphasis should be on the introduction of management accounting techniques, in general, and control techniques, in particular, that are consistent with the satisfaction of higher-level needs. This view is also shared by Caplan when he states that

> . . . it may be more important to concentrate on the development of organizational structures, leadership practices, and control systems which are consistent with satisfaction of the higher-level needs.[22]

3.2.2 Two-factor theory

In a series of studies, Herzberg and his associates developed the "motivation hygiene" theory.[23] Briefly, they found two factors affecting a job situation, which they labeled *satisfiers* and *dissatisfiers*. The satisfiers were related to the nature of the work itself and to rewards that flowed directly from the performance of that work. They were as follows: (1) perceived opportunity for achievement on the job, (2) recognition, (3) a sense of performing interesting and important work, (4) responsibility, and (5) advancement. The dissatisfiers were related to the context rather than the content of the job. They were as follows: (1) company policies that foster ineffectiveness, (2) incompetent supervision, (3) interpersonal relations, (4) working conditions, (5) salaries, (6) status, and (7) job security. The satisfiers were classified as "motivators" and the dissatisfiers as "hygiene" factors.

According to Herzberg, the satisfiers contribute very little to job dissatisfaction; and conversely, the dissatisfiers contribute very little to job satisfaction. Similarly, motivation to work is created by the satisfaction of the individual's needs for the satisfiers and not from an elimination of the dissatisfiers. The implications of Herzberg's theory for management accounting are twofold. First, to contribute to the motivation of employees, management accounting techniques should focus on better measurement and reporting of achievement, recognition, work, responsibility, and advancement. Second, given that the key to motivation is to make jobs more meaningful, management accounting techniques should focus on job enrichment. Job enrichment is the attempt by managers to design tasks in such a way as to affect employees' positive feelings about their job and to build in the opportunity for personal achievement, recognition, challenge, and personal growth. It gives the employees a greater amount of responsibility in carrying out complete tasks and insures a timely feedback on their performance.[24] Evans suggests several steps to insure job enrichment of relevance to management accounting:[25]

1. Eliminating controls from job while keeping accountability.
2. Increasing the individual's accountability for his or her job.
3. Providing each individual with a complete and natural work module (or elements of work).
4. Allowing greater job freedom for an individual's own work.
5. Providing timely feedbacks on performance to the employee instead of the supervisor.
6. Improving old tasks and introducing new tasks.
7. Assigning specific tasks so the employee can develop expertise in performing them.

3.2.3 Value/expectancy theory

The theories of Maslow, McClelland, and Herzberg are content theories in the sense that they attempt to identify what factors within the individual and the individual's environment induce high performance. The value/expectancy theory is a process theory in the sense that it attempts to explain and describe the process of how behavior is initiated, maintained, and terminated.

Originally developed by Lewin,[26] and later specially applied to motivation to work by Vroom,[27] the basic tenet of the value/expectancy theory is that an individual chooses personal behavior on the basis of: (1) expectations that such behavior will result in a specific outcome, and (2) the sum of the valences, i.e., personal utilities or rewards, derived from the outcome. Vroom advances the following theoretical proposition:

> The force on a person (motive) to perform a given act is based on the weighted value (or utility) of all the possible outcomes of the act multiplied by the perceived usefulness of the given act in the

attainment of these outcomes. Whenever an individual chooses between alternatives that involve certain outcomes, it seems clear that his behavior is affected not only by his preferences among outcomes, but also by the degree to which he believes these outcomes to be probable.[28]

Hence, an individual's motivation may be expressed as:

$$M = \Sigma[(E \rightarrow O)(V)]$$

where

E = Effort
O = Outcome
V = Values placed on the outcome

The above expression may be reformulated to include both an *effort-performance* linkage and a *performance-reward* linkage. The new model will include two expectancies. The first one refers to the probability that the effort will lead to a task accomplishment or performance. The second one refers to the probability that the task accomplishment will result in the desired outcomes. Hence, the individual's motivation may also be expressed as:

$$M = (E \rightarrow P)\Sigma[(P \rightarrow O)(V)]$$

where

P = performance

Porter and Lawler have extended the value/expectancy theory by arguing that poor performance may result if abilities are lacking and the individual's role perceptions are erroneous.[29] Thus, for preferences and expectations to affect performance, adequate ability and accurate role perceptions are necessary.

House's formulation of the model can be expressed as follows:[30]

$$M = IV_b + P_1(IV_a + \sum_{i=1}^{n} P_{2i}EV_i),$$
$$i = 1, 2, \ldots, n$$

where

M = Motivation to work

IV_a = Intrinsic valence associated with successful performance of the task

IV_b = Intrinsic valence associated with goal-directed behavior

EV_i = Extrinsic valences associated with the ith extrinsic reward contingent on work-goal accomplishment

P_l = The expectancy that goal-directed behavior will accomplish the work goal (a given level of specified performance); the measure's range is $(-1, +1)$

P_{2i} = The expectancy that work-goal accomplishment will lead to the ith extrinsic reward; the measure's range is $(-1, +1)$

This formulation shows some of the implications of expectancy theory for management accounting. Appropriate management accounting techniques may be chosen to affect the independent variables of the model in the following ways:

1. By determining what extrinsic rewards (EV_i) follow work-goal accomplishment.
2. By increasing through timely reports the individual's expectancy (P_2) that work-goal accomplishment leads to extrinsic rewards.
3. By increasing the intrinsic valence associated with work-goal accomplishment (IV_a) through a greater role of the individual in goal-setting and task-directed effort.
4. By recognizing and supporting the individual's effort thereby influencing P_l.
5. By increasing the net intrinsic valences associated with goal-directed behavior (IV_b).

3.2.4 Achievement theory

The concept of "achievement motive" was first introduced by McClelland, Atkinson, and their associates.[31] It is based on the desire of people to be challenged and to be innovative and adopt an "achievement-oriented behavior," i.e., a behavior directed toward meeting a standard of excellence. McClelland viewed the motive to achieve as distinct from acquisitiveness for money, except insofar as money is considered a symbol of achievement. Using the Thematic Appreciation Test (TAT) to measure three distinct needs (need for achievement, need for power, and need for affiliation), he found the achievement level to be correlated with personality and cultural variables.

The achievement-oriented individual likes to assume responsibility for individual achievement, seeks challenging tasks, takes calculated risks depending on the probabilitics of success. Therefore

> . . . he will take small risks for tasks serving as stepping stones for future rewards, take intermediate risks for tasks offering opportunities for achievement, and will attempt to find situations falling somewhere between the two extremes, providing the highest probability of success, and hence maximizing his sense of personal achievement.

According to the theory, the individuals will particularly behave in an achievement-oriented way in situations that enable them to strive for a standard of excellence, require the use of skills, present a challenge, and allow the individuals to appraise their performance. Accordingly, Atkinson stated that the strength of one's tendency to succeed at a task (T_s)

> . . . is a multiplicative function of three variables: motive to achieve success (M_S) which is conceived as a relatively general and stable disposition of personality and measured in terms of need for achievement; and two other variables which represent the effect of the immediate environment—the strength

of expectancy (or subjective probability) that performance of a task will be followed by success (P_s) and the relative attractiveness of success of that particular activity, which is called the incentive value of success (I_s). I_s assumed to be greater the more difficult the task.[32]

Another important contention of the theory is that all motives are learned, including the achievement motive. As a result, the high achiever is experienced in making maximizing decisions, is less affected by anxiety, and proceeds in an efficient way in any endeavor.

What these contentions imply for management accounting is: (1) the necessity of constructing ways of developing the achievement motive at all managerial levels, and (2) the need to introduce management accounting techniques and to report management accounting information which encourages and facilitates the performance of high achievers.

3.2.5 Inequity theory

Elaine Walster, Stacey Adams, and their colleagues have advanced that individuals in a relationship have two motives: to maximize their own gains and to maintain equity in the relationship.[33] Inequity results when a person's rewards from a relationship are not proportional to what that person has put in the relationship. More explicitly, inequity theory is based on the premise that when individuals compare their own situations with other situations and have a feeling of inequity, in terms of feeling either underrewarded or overrewarded for their contributions, they experience increased tension and strive to reduce it. Hence, overpaid workers will increase their efforts by producing more as a way of reducing inequity, while underpaid workers will produce less to achieve a contribution-reward balance. Other methods of restoring equity may be used also. Walster et al. state that individuals can restore *actual equity* by altering either their own payoffs or those of other participants. Similarly, a *psychological equity* can be restored when individuals change their perceptions of either rewards or contributions so that their contributions appear greater or lower than originally thought. They may also restore equity by quitting their job, severing the relationship with the comparison person, or by forcing the comparison person to leave the field.

The inequity theory suggests, then, that rewards must appear to the employees to be fair or equitable. An appeal to equity norms can be used to reduce conflict. The role of management accounting in restoring equity is in insuring correct and accurate measurement and reporting of performance and the corresponding rewards. To avoid creating feelings of inequity, the methods of measuring performance and rewards should be made public to the employees.

3.3 MODELS OF DECISION MAKING

Management accounting necessitates a good grasp of decision making in organizations. The identification of the decision-making models most relevant to particular contexts and most preferred by particular individuals allows the management accountant to adapt the services to offer to the realities of the decision situation. The literature on decision making identifies five main perspectives: the "rational" manager view, the "satisficing" process-oriented view, the organizational procedures view, the political view, and the individual differences perspective.[34]

Before analyzing each of these models, it is appropriate to mention the excellent analysis of the Cuban missile crisis by G. T. Allison using three of these models: the "rational" actor view, the organizational procedures view, and the political view.[35] Addressing the central issues of the crisis from one of the three perspectives, "lead[s] one to see, emphasize, and worry about quite different aspects of events."[36] By analogy, addressing management issues from any of the five perspectives leads one to have different perceptions and understanding of events and place on the management accountant different demands for services. Let us then examine each of these models and its importance to management accounting.

3.3.1 The rational view

The rational view of decision making is a normative model that refers to a consistent value-maximizing choice process in the presence of specific constraints. This process may be summarized as follows:

1. Individuals assume that there is a set of alternative acts or courses of action displayed before them in a particular situation.
2. They associate a set of possible outcomes or consequences with the set of possible acts.
3. They have a preference ordering over the consequences or payoff function that allows them to rank the consequences and select that act which ranks highest in their payoff function.

This view is used and relied upon as the model of the "economic man" in neoclassical economic theory and as the model of the "rational man" in game theory and statistical decision theory. Both make optimal choices in the presence of well-defined specific constraints.

As a defense of the rational view of decision making, one of two assumptions has been made. On the one hand, there is the assumption of *comprehensive rationality* where individuals have perfect knowledge of all alternative acts, all the consequences, and the corresponding payoff function. On the other hand, there is the assumption of *limited rationality* with its inherent restricted claim on "optimal choice." Whatever the assumptions, the rational view of decision making requires the management accountant to define all the possibilities in terms of acts, consequences, and payoff function, and to evaluate the costs and benefits associated with rational decision making.

The rational view of decision making, although normative and rigorous, has been criticized as being descriptively unrealistic. Simon, in particular, advanced the principle of *bounded rationality* of the human decision maker:

> When the limits to rationality are viewed from the individual's standpoint, they fall into three categories: he is limited by unconscious skills, habits, and reflexes; he is limited by his values and conceptions of purpose, which may diverge from the organizational goals; he is limited by the extent of his knowledge and information. The individual can be rational in terms of the organization's goals only to the extent that he is *able* to pursue a particular course of action, he has a correct conception of the *goal* of the action, and he is correctly *informed* about the conditions surrounding his action. Within the boundaries laid down by these factors, his choices are rational-goal oriented.[37]

In replacement of the "economic man," Simon suggests the notion of the "administrative" or "satisficing" man as more representative of what is in decision making.

3.3.2 The satisficing and process-oriented view

The satisficing and process-oriented view of decision making is a descriptive model which maintains that the administrative individual *satisfices* rather than optimizes when making most decisions. Thus, rather than searching the haystack for the sharpest needle, the objective of the administrative man is to find one sharp enough to sew with.[38] Simon summarizes the assumptions of the satisficer's theory as follows:

> In actual organizational practice, no one attempts to find an optimal solution for the whole problem. Instead, various particular decisions, or groups of decisions, within the whole complex are made by specialized members or units of the organization. In making these particular decisions, the specialized units

> do not solve the whole problem but find a "satisfactory" solution for one or more subproblems, where some of the effects of the solution on other parts of the system are incorporated in the definition of "satisfactory."[39]

Thus, the satisficing man makes decision-making choice in context of a simplified view of the real situation. Simon introduces a concept of "subjective rationality" as a challenge to the concept of "objective rationality" advocated by the rational view of decision making. Subjective rationality depends on the individual's personal values. Thus, an objectively rational decision calls for a maximizing behavior given values in a given situation, while a subjectively rational decision calls for maximizing attainment relative to the actual knowledge of the individual.[40] To be able to satisfice, the individual's strategies will consist essentially of heuristics or rules of thumb that meet a subjective minimum standard with respect to the things being sought.

That managers satisfice rather than optimize, refer to subjective rather than objective rationality, and rely on their heuristics places distinctive demands on the management accountant. To be able to service managers and facilitate their decision-making process, an understanding of their heuristics is essential. It is not an insurmountable task, given the general evidence suggesting how simple and how few are the heuristics used by managers. It also implies a good working relationship between managers and management accountants.

3.3.3 The organizational procedures view

The organizational procedures view of decision making is a descriptive model which maintains that individuals comply with and act according to a fixed set of standard operating procedures and programs. They make their choice in terms of goals and on the basis of expectations. Cyert and March perceive the organization as a coalition of individuals with different demands, priorities, goals, focus of attention, and competencies.[41] Decision making within the organization requires bargaining among the coalition members resulting in de facto agreements and standard procedures for dealing with problematic situations.

Thus, individuals will act according to standard patterns of behavior established in their particular organizational unit to achieve its stated goals. What results in the organization is: (1) a permanent goal conflict between the units with possibly the dominant coalition imposing its independent constraints, (2) a quasi-resolution of conflict marked by a sequential attention to problems, (3) uncertainty avoidance, (4) problematic search where search is triggered by a specific problem and motivated to finding a solution to the problem, and (5) organizational learning leading to changes in goals, expectations, and standard procedures.

This process-oriented view of decision making has been applied with some success to simulate the working of a retail department store by Cyert and March,[42] the trust investment process used by trust officers in a bank by Clarkson,[43] the behavior of government units in municipal budgeting by Crecine,[44] and the foreign investment decision process of businesses by Aharoni.[45]

That managers may belong to coalitions which rely on programs and standard procedures places distinctive demands on management accountants. These coalitions and their standard procedures should be identified by management accountants so to be able to service managers and facilitate their decision making. This implies that management accountants must be careful not to be identified with any of these coalitions, but as support agents providing the necessary information for an efficient resolution of problems. Following Lawrence and Lorsch's[46] appeal for a balance between integration and differentiation within complex organizations, management accountants may act as integrating agents between the subunits of the organization.

3.3.4 The political view

The political view of decision making is a descriptive model which maintains that decisions are due partly to political processes. In this process, different groups committed to different courses of action interact and arrive at decisions through the "pulling and hauling that is politics."[47] The differences between this view and the rational and process views are summarized by Allison as follows:

> . . . what moves the chess pieces is not simply the reasons that support a course of action or the routines of organizations that enact an alternative but the power and skill of proponents and opponents of the action in itself.[48]

Thus, each individual in the firm is a player in a competitive game called politics, where persuasion, accommodation, bargaining, and the constant search for support are the determinants of decision making. This may be justified because

> . . . managers (government leaders) have competitive, not homogeneous interests; priorities and perceptions are shaped by positions; problems are much more varied than straightforward strategic issues; management of piecemeal streams of decisions is more important than steady-state choices; making sure that management (the government) does what is decided is more difficult than selecting the preferred solution.[49] (Allison's original words are shown in parentheses.)

This political view resulted in the concept of incremental change advanced mainly by Lindblom.[50] According to this view, labeled as "the art of the possible," managers attack rather than solve problems incrementally and through "successive limited comparisons."

That managers may be motivated by political positions and disagree with other political positions in the firm, that they may favor managing through incremental muddling rather than comprehensive, satisfactory, or procedural choice is very relevant for the management accountant and should not be ignored. The acceptance and use of either management accounting techniques or information suggested by the management accountant is very much a function of the political dimensions existing in the firm.

3.3.5 The individual differences view

The individual differences view maintains that individuals have specific decision-making styles appropriate for some cases and less so for others. This view emerged from the recognition in psychology of the concept of cognitive style as a hypothetical construct to explain the mediation process between stimuli and responses. Five approaches have been reported for the study of cognitive style: authoritarianism, dogmatism, cognitive complexity, integrative complexity, and field dependence.[51]

1. Authoritarianism arose from the focus by Adorno et al. on the relationship between personality, antidemocratic attitudes, and behavior.[52] They were primarily interested in individuals whose way of thinking made them susceptible to antidemocratic propaganda. Two of the behavioral correlates of authoritarianism, rigidity and intolerance of ambiguity, were reflections of an underlying cognitive style. For example, Dermer investigated the relationship between intolerance of ambiguity and subjective cue usage.[53] His result showed a significant positive correlation between intolerance of ambiguity and the amount of information perceived to be important.

2. Dogmatism arose from Rokeach's efforts to develop a structurally-based measure of authoritarianism to replace the content-based measure developed by Adorno and his colleagues.[54] His interest was in developing a measure of cognitive style which would be independent of the content of thought.

3. Cognitive complexity as introduced by Kelly[55] and Bieri et al.[56] focuses on the psychological dimensions that individuals

use to structure their environments and to differentiate the behavior of others. The more cognitively complex individuals are assumed to have a greater number of dimensions available with which to construe the behavior of others than the less cognitively complex persons. Another clarification of decision makers in the literature is made in terms of two cognitive styles: *heuristic* and *analytic*. Based on terms and meanings used by Huysmans,[57] they may be defined as follows: Analytic decision makers reduce problem situations to a more or less explicit, often quantitative, model as a basis for their decision. Heuristic decision makers refer instead to common sense, intuition, and unquantified feelings about future development as they apply to the totality of the situation as an organic whole rather than as built from clearly identifiable parts. Huysmans's findings show particularly that cognitive style may operate as an effective constraint on the implementation of operations research recommendations, and that operations researchers perceive their own analytic style as self-evident and tend to ignore the impact of cognitive style on the acceptance and use of analytic techniques. Similarly, in an experimental study of the relationship between different information structures, decision approaches, and learning patterns, Mock, Estrin, and Vasarhelyi[58] found that analytics significantly outperformed heuristics in terms of profit and decision time.

4. Integrative complexity as presented by Harvey et al.,[59] and later expanded by Schroder et al.,[60] results from the view that people engage in two activities in processing sensory input: *differentiation* and *integration*. Differentiation refers to the individual's ability to place stimuli along dimensions. Integration refers to the individual's ability to employ complex rules to combine these dimensions. Then a person low on both activities is said to be *concrete,* while a person high on both activities is said to be *abstract*. The continuum from concrete to abstract is referred to as integrative or conceptual complexity. To the concept

of integrative complexity is usually added the concept of environmental complexity and the level of information processing. It is expressed by the "U-Curve Hypothesis" as depicted in Exhibit 3.1. As the level of environmental complexity increases, the level of information processing increases and reaches a maximum level at an optimal level of environmental complexity beyond which it begins to decrease.[61] Schroder et al. extended the concept of the inverted U-shaped curve to the study of integrative complexity. The differences between the concrete and the abstract individual are also shown in Exhibit 3.1. The more abstract the individual, the higher the maximum level of information processing.

5. Finally, field dependence as presented by Witkin and his associates is a measure of the extent of differentiation in the area of perception.[62] Field dependent individuals tend to perceive the overall organization of a field and are relatively unable to perceive parts of the field as discrete. Field independent individuals, however, tend to perceive parts of the field as discrete from organized parts rather than fused with it.

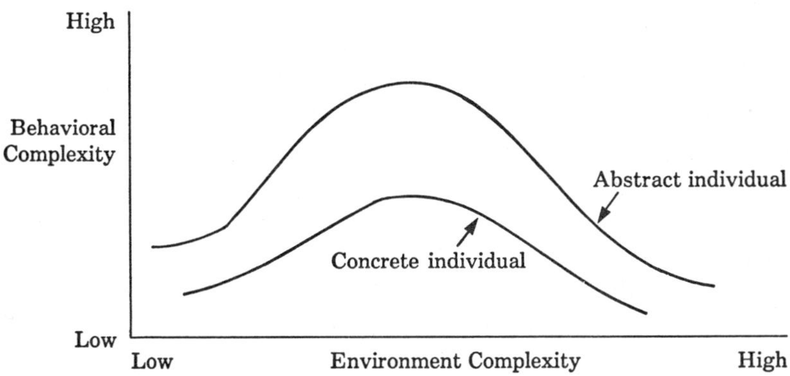

Exhibit 3.1 Functioning of concrete and abstract individuals in relation to environmental complexity

That managers have specific cognitive styles in terms of authoritarianism, dogmatism, cognitive complexity, integrative complexity, and field dependence which give them specific styles of decision making has strong implications for management accounting. First, management accounting reports should be compatible with the cognitive structures of its users. They should be designed on the basis of realistic assumptions about the users' decision styles. Second, the utilization and the acceptance of management accounting techniques and information depend on their suitability to the cognitive style of the users. Thus, management accountants should be aware of the cognitive style constraint in the implementation of management accounting. Quantitative-based management accounting techniques may be more attractive to the analytic rather than the heuristic decision makers. Finally, the analytic management accountants should not assume that all users are and should be like themselves.

3.4 CONCLUSIONS

Management accounting rests on behavioral foundations. The type of objective function, motivation theories, and the different models of decision making identify the factors likely to affect the behavior and performance of an individual within the organization (See Exhibit 3.2.) First, management may either adopt the stockholder wealth maximization model, the managerial welfare model, or the social welfare model. The adoption of any model defines and restricts management to specific management techniques, attitudes, and behavior conducive to the accomplishment of the given objective. Second, the theories of motivation, namely, the need theory, the two-factor theory, the value/expectancy theory, the achievement theory, and the inequity theory, identify what environmental factors and management accounting techniques are susceptible to activate high performance or explain and describe the process of how desirable

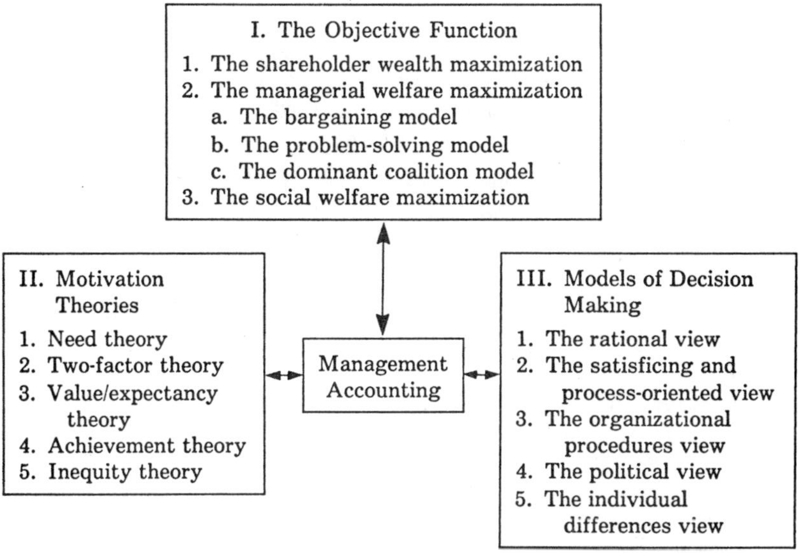

Exhibit 3.2 The behavioral foundations of management accounting

behavior may be initiated, encouraged, and even stopped. Finally, the identification of the decision-making models used by users in specific contexts may be of great help to the management accountant in adapting services to the users and the specific contexts. Five main perspectives of decision making were examined: the "rational" view, the "satisficing" process-oriented view, the organizational procedures view, the political view, and the individual differences view.

ENDNOTES

1. Amitai Etzioni, *Modern Organizations* (Englewood Cliffs, N.J.: Prentice-Hall, Inc., 1964), p. 3.
2. Richard H. Hall, *Organizations: Structure and Process* (Englewood Cliffs, N.J.: Prentice-Hall, Inc., 1972), p. 9.

3. V. Buck, "The Organization as a System of Constraints," *Approaches to Organization Design,* ed. J. D. Thompson (Pittsburgh: The University of Pittsburgh Press, 1966), p. 109.
4. J. D. Thompson, *Organizations in Action* (New York: McGraw-Hill Book Company, 1967), p. 128.
5. C. Perrow, "The Analysis of Goals in Complex Organizations," *American Sociological Review* 26 (1961): 854–66.
6. Etzioni, *Modern Organizations,* p. 7.
7. Chapman M. Findlay and G. A. Whitmore, "Beyond Shareholder Wealth Maximization," *Financial Management* (Winter 1974): 25–35.
8. E. Solomon, *The Theory of Financial Management* (New York: Columbia University Press, 1963), p. 24.
9. W. Baumol, *Business Behavior, Value and Growth* (New York: Macmillan Co., 1964).
10. R. Marris, *The Economic Theory of Managerial Capitalism* (London: Macmillan Co., 1964).
11. A. Papandreou, "Some Basic Issues in the Theory of the Firm," *A Survey of Contemporary Economics,* ed. B. Haley (Homewood, Ill.: Richard D. Irwin, Inc., 1952). Also, O. Williamson, *The Economics of Discretionary Behavior: Managerial Objectives in the Theory of the Firm* (Englewood Cliffs, N.J.: Prentice-Hall, Inc., 1964).
12. B. Branch, "Corporate Objectives and Market Performance," *Financial Management* (Summer 1973): 24–29.
13. Francine S. Hall, "Organizational Goals: The Status of Theory and Research," *Managerial Accounting: The Behavioral Foundations,* ed. J. Leslie Livingstone (Columbus, Ohio: Grid, Inc., 1975), pp. 1–29.
14. For an excellent presentation of these models, the reader is advised to examine the article by Hall mentioned in the preceding footnote.
15. Ibid., p. 17.
16. Ibid., p. 20.
17. Ibid., p. 23.
18. American Accounting Association, Committee on Measurement of Social Costs, "Report of the Committee on the Measurement of Social Costs," *The Accounting Review,* Supplement to Vol. 69 (1974): 100.

19. Ibid., pp. 101–02.
20. M. R. Jones, ed., *Nebraska Symposium on Motivation* (Lincoln: University of Nebraska Press, 1955), p. 14.
21. A. Maslow, "A Dynamic Theory of Human Motivation," *Psychological Review* 50 (1943): 370–73.
22. E. H. Caplan, *Management Accounting and Behavioral Science* (Reading, Mass.: Addison-Wesley Publishing Company, 1971), p. 49.
23. F. Herzberg; B. Mausner; and B. Snyderman, *The Motivation to Work,* 2nd ed. (New York: Wiley & Sons, 1959).
24. Jacques E. Powers, "Job Enrichment: How One Company Overcame the Obstacle," *Personnel* (May–June 1972): 8.
25. Martin G. Evans, "Herzberg's Two Factor Theory of Motivation," *Personnel Journal* (January 1970): p. 33.
26. K. Lewin, *Field Theory and Social Science* (New York: Harper, 1951).
27. V. H. Vroom, *Work and Motivation* (New York: Wiley & Sons, 1964).
28. Ibid., p. 18.
29. L. W. Porter and E. E. Lawler, *Managerial Attitudes and Performance* (Homewood, Ill.: Irwin-Dorsey, 1968).
30. R. J. House, "A Path-Goal Theory of Leader Effectiveness," *Administrative Science Quarterly* 16 (September 1971): 321–38.
31. D. C. McClelland, *Personality* (New York: William Sloan, 1951); *The Achieving Society* (New York: Van Nostrand, 1961). Also, J. W. Atkinson, "Toward Experimental Analysis of Human Motivation in Terms of Motives, Expectancies, and Incentives," *Motives in Fantasy, Action and Society,* ed. J. W. Atkinson (New York: Van Nostrand, 1958).
32. J. W. Atkinson, "Motivational Determinants of Risk Taking Behavior," *Psychological Review* 64 (1957): 14.
33. E. Walster; E. Berscheid; and G. W. Walster, "New Directions in Equity Research," *Journal of Personality and Social Psychology* 25 (1973): 151–76. Also, J. S. Adams, "Toward an Understanding of Inequity, "*Journal of Abnormal and Social Psychology* 22 (1968): 1045–53.
34. Peter G. Keen and Michael S. Scott Morton, *Decision Support Systems: An Organizational Perspective,* Addison-Wesley Series

on Decision Support (Reading, Mass.: Addison-Wesley Publishing Company, Inc., 1978), pp. 62–63.
35. G. T. Allison, *Essence of a Decision* (Boston, Mass.: Little, Brown, 1971).
36. Ibid., p. v.
37. Herbert A. Simon, *Administrative Behavior,* 2nd ed. (New York: Macmillan, 1957), p. 241.
38. J. G. March and H. A. Simon, *Organizations* (New York: Wiley, 1958), p. 141.
39. Simon, *Administrative Behavior,* p. 272.
40. Ibid., p. 76.
41. R. M. Cyert and J. G. March, *A Behavioral Theory of the Firm* (Englewood Cliffs, N.J.: Prentice-Hall, 1963).
42. Ibid.
43. G. E. Clarkson, "A Model of Trust Investment Behavior" in *A Behavioral Theory of the Firm,* Ch. 10.
44. John P. Crecine, "Governmental Problem Solving" in *A Computer Simulation of Municipal Budgeting* (New York, 1969).
45. Lair Aharoni, *The Foreign Investment Decision Process* (Boston, 1966).
46. P. R. Lawrence and J. W. Lorsch, *Organization and Environment* (Cambridge, Mass.: Division of Research, Harvard Business School, 1967).
47. Allison, *Essence of a Decision,* p. 144.
48. Ibid., p. 145.
49. Ibid., p. 146.
50. C. W. Lindblom, "The Science of Muddling Through," *Public Administration Review* (Spring 1959): 79–88.
51. Kenneth R. Goldstein and Sheldon Blackman, *Cognitive Style: Five Approaches and Relevant Research* (New York: John Wiley and Sons, 1978), pp. 12–13.
52. T. W. Adorno; E. Frenkel-Brunswick; D. J. Levinson; and R. N. Sanford, *The Authoritarian Personality* (New York: Harper and Row, 1950).
53. J. Dermer, "Cognitive Characteristics and the Perceived Importance of Information," *The Accounting Review* (January 1973): 511–19.
54. M. Rokeach, *The Open and Closed Mind* (New York: Basic Books, 1960).

55. G. A. Kelly, *The Psychology of Personal Constructs,* 2 vols. (New York: Norton, 1955).
56. J. Bieri, "Cognitive Complexity and Personality Development," *Experience, Structure and Adaptability,* ed. O. J. Harvey (New York: Springer, 1966).
57. Jan H. B. Huysmans, "The Effectiveness of the Cognitive-Style Constraint in Implementing Operations Research Proposals," *Management Science* (September 1970): 94–95.
58. T. Mock; T. Estrin; and M. Vasarhelyi, "Learning Patterns, Decision Approach and Value of Information," *Journal of Accounting Research* (Spring 1972): 129–53.
59. O. J. Harvey; D. E. Hunt; and H. M. Schroder, *Conceptual Systems and Personality Organizations* (New York: John Wiley and Sons, 1961).
60. H. M. Schroder; M. J. Driver; and S. Streufert, *Human Information Processing* (New York: Holt, Rinehart and Winston, 1967).
61. Ibid., p. 37.
62. H. A. Witkin; R. B. Dyks; H. F. Faterson; D. R. Goodenough; and S. A. Karyn, *Psychological Differentiation* (New York: Wiley, 1962). Also, H. A. Witkin; H. B. Lewis; M. Hertzman; K. Machover; P. B. Meisner; and S. Wagner, *Personality Through Perception* (New York: Harper, 1954).

BIBLIOGRAPHY

The objective function

Anthony, Robert N. "The Trouble with Profit Maximization." *Harvard Business Review* (Nov.–Dec. 1960): 126–34.

Beams, Floyd A., and Fertig, Paul E. "Pollution Control Through Social Cost Conversion." *The Journal of Accountancy* (November 1971): 37–42.

Belkaoui, Ahmed. "The Impact of the Disclosure of the Environmental Effects of Organizational Behavior on the Market." *Financial Management* (Winter 1976): 26–31.

Cyert, Richard M.; March, James G.; and Starbuck, William H. "Two Experiments on Bias and Conflict in Organizational Estimation." *Management Science* (April 1961): 254–64.

Donaldson, Gordon. "Financial Goals: Management Versus Stockholders." *Harvard Business Review* (May–June 1963): 116–29.

Estes, Ralph W. "Accounting for Social Costs." *The Accounting Review* (April 1972): 284–90.

Findlay, M. Chapman, and Witmore, G. A. "Beyond Shareholder Wealth Maximization." *Financial Management* (Winter 1974): 25–35.

Lewellen, Wilbur G. "Management and Ownership in the Large Firm." *Journal of Finance* (May 1969): 299–322.

Linowes, David F. "Socio-Economic Accounting." *The Journal of Accountancy* (November 1968): 37–42.

Livingstone, J. Leslie, ed. *Managerial Accounting: The Behavioral Foundations* (Columbus, Ohio: Grid, Inc., 1975).

Mobley, Sybil C. "The Challenges of Socio-Economic Accounting." *The Accounting Review* (October 1970): 762–68.

Schiff, Michael, and Lewin, Arie T. "Where Traditional Budgeting Fails." *Financial Executive* (May 1968): 55–62.

Wiliamson, O. *The Economics of Discretionary Behavior: Managerial Objectives in the Theory of the Firm* (Englewood Cliffs, N.J.: Prentice-Hall, Inc., 1964).

Motivation theories

Adams, J. S. "Toward an Understanding of Inequity." *Journal of Abnormal and Social Psychology* 22 (1968): 1045–53.

Caplan, E. H. *Management Accounting and Behavioral Science* (Reading, Mass.: Addison-Wesley Publishing Company, 1971).

Chung, Kae H. "Toward a General Theory of Motivation and Performance." *California Management Review* (Spring 1969): 81–88.

Herzberg, F.; Mausner, B.; and Snyderman, B. *The Motivation to Work,* 2nd ed. (New York: John Wiley and Sons, 1959).

Maslow, A. "A Dynamic Theory of Human Motivation." *Psychological Review* 50 (1943): 370–73.

McClelland, D. C. *The Achieving Society* (New York: Van Nostrand, 1961).

Porter, L. W., and Lawler, E. E. *Managerial Attitudes and Performance* (Irwin-Dorsey, 1968).

Schein, Edgar. *Organization Psychology,* 2nd ed. (Englewood Cliffs, N.J.: Prentice-Hall, 1970).

Vinacke, W. E. "Motivation as a Complex Problem." *Nebraska Symposium on Motivation* (Lincoln: University of Nebraska Press, 1962).

Vroom, V. H. *Work and Motivation* (New York: John Wiley and Sons, 1964).

Walster, E.; Berscheid, E.; and Walster, G. W. "New Directions in Equity Research." *Journal of Personality and Social Psychology* 25 (1973): 151–76.

Models of decision making

Allison, G. T. *Essence of a Decision* (Boston, Mass.: Little, Brown, 1971).

Bariff, M. L., and Lusk, E. J. "Cognitive and Personality Tests for the Design of Management Information Systems." *Management Science* (April 1977): 820–29.

Cyert, R. M., and March, J. G. *A Behavioral Theory of the Firm* (Englewood Cliffs, N.J.: Prentice-Hall, 1963).

Dermer, J. "Cognitive Characteristics and the Perceived Importance of Information." *The Accounting Review* (January 1973): 511–19.

Goldstein, Kenneth, and Blackman, Sheldon. *Cognitive Style: Five Approaches and Relevant Research* (New York: John Wiley and Sons, 1978).

Huysmans, Jan H. B. "The Effectiveness of the Cognitive-Style Constraint in Implementing Operations Research Proposals." *Management Science* (September 1970): 92–104.

Keen, Peter G., and Scott Morton, Michael S. *Decision Support Systems: An Organizational Perspective* (Addison-Wesley Series on Decision Support) Reading, Mass.: Addison-Wesley Publishing Company, Inc., 1978.

Lindblom, C. W. "The Science of Muddling Through." *Public Administrative Review* (Spring 1959): 79–88.

March, J. G., and Simon, H. A. *Organizations* (New York: John Wiley and Sons, 1958).

Schroder, H. M.; Driver, M. J.; and Streufert, S. *Human Information Processing* (New York: Holt, Rinehart and Winston, 1967).

Simon, Herbert A. *Administrative Behavior,* 2nd ed. (New York: Macmillan Co., 1957).

Sorter, George H.; Becker, Selwyn W.; Archibald, T. R.; and Beaver, W. "Corporate Personality as Reflected in Accounting Decisions: Some Preliminary Findings." *Journal of Accounting Research* (Autumn 1964): 183–96.

Chapter Four

THE DECISIONAL FOUNDATIONS

A fundamental objective of management accounting is to facilitate and support all the aspects of an organization's decision making. To accomplish this objective, management accountants should be aware of the kinds and levels of decisions involved in order to identify those particular areas where management accounting techniques and information would be most relevant and useful. For this purpose, different conceptual frameworks for viewing decisions and decision systems have been proposed in the management accounting and information systems literature. They provide a good basis for viewing the types of decisions and decision systems, the types of information needed, and the role of management accounting.

4.1 ANTHONY FRAMEWORK

Although a typology of managerial activities, Anthony framework may also be conceived as a hierarchy of decision systems, each requiring different planning and control systems. The decision systems are categorized as strategic planning, management control, and operational control.[1]

Strategic planning as defined by Anthony is "the process of deciding on objectives of the organization, on changes in these objectives, on the resources used to attain these objectives, and on the policies that are to govern the acquisition, use, and disposition of resources."[2] The main concern of the strategic planner is the relationship between the organization and its environment. This concern is expressed in the formulation of a long-range plan that defines the intended future orientation of the firm. Strategic planning is the responsibility of senior managers and analysts who will approach problems on an ad hoc basis as the need for a solution arises.

Management control is "the process by which managers assure that resources are obtained and used effectively and efficiently in the accomplishment of the organization's objectives."[3] The concern is with the conduct of managerial activities within the framework established by strategic planning. These activities require sometimes subjective interpretations and involve personal interactions. Management control involves both top management and the middle managers who will approach problems following a definite pattern and timetable to insure efficient and effective results.

Operational control is "the process of assuring that specific tasks are carried out effectively and efficiently."[4] The concern is with individual tasks or transactions. The performance of these tasks or transactions is accomplished according to rules and procedures derived from management control. These rules and procedures are often expressed in terms of a mathematical model.

Although, as recognized by Anthony, the boundaries between the three categories are often not clear, they are useful for the analysis of the different activities and their information requirements. The decision categories form a continuum and require different information. Exhibit 4.1 summarizes the information requirements by decision category.

Anthony's framework has the advantage of simplicity, and it facilitates communications between individuals in the organization by categorizing different types of decisions and their information requirements. For management accounting, it implies a tailoring of the data produced to the context and category of the particular decision. It also calls for different approaches to planning and control in each of the strategic planning, management control, and operational control areas.

4.2 SIMON FRAMEWORK

Similar to Anthony's framework, Simon's framework presents a taxonomy of decisions.[5] However, while Anthony's framework focuses on the purpose of decision-making activity (strategic planning, management control, and operational control),

Information Attribute	Strategic Planning	Management Control	Operational Control
Source	Externally generated	Mostly internally generated	Internally generated
Accuracy	Accurate in magnitude only	Accurate within decision bounds	Very accurate
Scope	Summary data	Moderately detailed data	Detailed data
Frequency	Periodically reported	Regularly reported	Frequently reported
Time span	Long range	Medium range	Short range
Organization	Loose	Structured	Highly structured
Type of information	Qualitative	Mixed	Quantitative
Age of information	Old	Mixed	Current
Characteristic	Unique to problem	Exception reporting	Repetitive
Nature	Relates to establishment of broad policies	Relates to the achievement of organizational objectives	Relates to a specific task

Exhibit 4.1 Information requirements by decision category

Simon's framework focuses on the question of problem solving by individuals regardless of their position within an organization.

Simon maintains that all problem solving can be broken down into three distinct phases: intelligence, design, and choice. Intelligence consists of surveying the environment for situations that demand decisions. It implies an identification of the problem(s), the collection of information, and the establishment of goals and evaluative criteria. Design involves delineating and analyzing various courses of action for the problems identified in the intelligence phase. It implies an enumeration and combination of feasible alternatives and their evaluation on the basis of the criteria established in the intelligence phase. Choice involves the choice of the best alternative. Although not mentioned by Simon, decision making involves a fourth phase, implementation, designed to insure proper execution of choice.

Simon's framework makes also the distinction between programmed and nonprogrammed decisions:

> Decisions are programmed to the extent that they are repetitive and routine, to the extent that a definite procedure has been worked out for handling them so that they don't have to be treated *de novo* each time they occur. Decisions are nonprogrammed to the extent that they are novel, unstructured, and consequential. There is no cut-and-dried method of handling the problem because it hasn't arisen before, or because its precise nature and structure are elusive or complex, or because it is so important that it deserves a custom-tailored treatment. . . . By nonprogrammed I mean a response where the system has no specific procedure to deal with situations like the one at hand, but must fall back on whatever general capacity it has for intelligent, adaptive, problem-oriented action.[6]

Because they are repetitive and routine, programmed decisions require little time in the design phase. On the other hand, nonprogrammed decisions require much more time in the design phase. In general, the terms *structured* and *unstructured* are used for programmed and nonprogrammed to imply less dependence on the computer and to show more dependence on the basic character of the problem-solving activity in question. The two classifications advanced by Simon may be viewed as polar types for a continuum of decision-making activity. For example, "semi-structured" decisions may be those for which one or two of the intelligence, design, and choice phases are unstructured.

That decisions may fall on a continuum going from structured to unstructured has implications for management accounting. Structured decisions are solvable by analytic techniques, while unstructured decisions generally are not. The analytic techniques required for the structured decisions may be either based on clerical routine and habit or formalized techniques from operations research and electronic data processing. The decision techniques required for unstructured decisions may be either based on human intuition and judgment or heuristic techniques. While the role of management accounting for structured decisions appears without doubt to be one of providing and assisting in the use of fixed routines, it is not very obvious in the case of unstructured decisions. Users may rely more on their decision style, intuition, or heuristics for the unstructured decisions or tasks.

4.3 GORRY-SCOTT MORTON FRAMEWORK

As mentioned earlier, Anthony's framework is based on the purpose of the decision-making activity, while Simon's framework is based on the methods or techniques of problem solving. The Gorry and Scott Morton framework provides a combination of both frameworks in the form of a matrix that classifies decisions on both a structured-to-unstructured dimension and on an operational-to-strategic dimension.[7] Exhibit 4.2 shows an expanded example of the matrix obtained from the synthesis provided by Gorry and Scott Morton.

	Operational Control	Management Control	Strategic Planning
	Accounts receivable	Budgeting	Tanker fleet mix
	Order entry	Short-term forecasting	Warehouse and plant location
Structured	Inventory reordering	Engineered costs	
		Linear programming for manufacturing	
	Inventory control	Variance analysis	Mergers and acquisitions
Semi-Structured	Production scheduling	Overall budget	Capital acquisition analysis
	Bond trading	Budget preparation	New product planning
	Cash management	Hiring personnel	R and D planning
Unstructured	PERT COST systems	Sales and production	

Exhibit 4.2 An expanded example of Gorry and Scott Morton framework

The implications for management accounting from both the Anthony and Simon frameworks apply to the Gorry and Scott Morton framework. The synthesis, however, presents additional implications. First, different information requirements and different methods of data collection and maintenance are required not only for the three decision categories borrowed from Anthony, but also for the types of decisions borrowed from Simon. This implies that the design of a management accounting support system is flexible enough to cope with the various complex demands. For example, in the structured case, the goal of management accounting may be to facilitate the processing of information; while in the unstructured case, it may be to improve the organization and presentation of information inputs.[8] Second, different organizational structures, different managerial skills and talents, and different numbers of managers may be required for each decision category. The decision process, the implementation process, and the level of analytic sophistication will differ among the three decision categories and call for different organization structures:

> . . . on strategic problems, a task force reporting to the user and virtually independent of the computer group may make sense. The important issues are problem definition and problem structure; the implementation and computer issues are relatively simple by comparison. In management control, the single user, although still dominant in his application, has problems of interfacing with other users. An organizational design that encourages cross-functional (marketing, production, distribution, etc.) cooperation is probably desirable. In operational control, the organizational design should include the user as a major influence, but he will have to be balanced with operational systems experts, and the whole group can quite possibly stay within functional boundaries.[9]

Finally, the model requirements may be different between the three areas, given the differences in the information requirements, the frequency of decisions in each area, and their relative magnitude. The operational control system calls for frequent decisions, and the models for these decisions need to be "efficient in running time, have ready access to current data, and be structured so as to be easily changed."[10] The models in strategic planning, and to a lesser extent management control, are infrequent, individual, and dependent on the managers involved.

While not referring to management accounting per se, but to a more general information systems concept labeled "Decision Support Systems," Keen and Scott Morton identified several implications of the framework to the design and implementation of a decision support system:

1. The skills and attitudes of the *people* involved in building a DSS (decision support system) for semi-structured decisions need to differ from those building similar systems for structured decisions.
2. Ill-structured problems require a different *technology* to support decisions than structured problems.
3. While a well-structured operational control problem may require the use of optimization algorithms, most other problems will rely on different *models*.
4. The design of a DSS should be accomplished through a continuous evolutionary *process* to accommodate future needs, learning and growth.[11]

Because management accounting is a decision support system, the above implications apply also to it. It requires people with different skills and attitudes, different technologies, different models, and different processes to accommodate both structured and unstructured decisions on one hand and strategic planning, management control, and operational control on the other hand.

4.4 FORRESTER FRAMEWORK

As developed by Professor Jay Forrester, the essence of *industrial dynamics* is that social systems such as business organizations can be understood through nonlinear feedback systems concepts.[12] Any system is characterized by its closed-loop (information feedback) structure. He describes the state of the organization by information on the *levels* of various variables in the organization, such as inventory, manpower, open orders, money, sales, etc. The activity in the organization takes the form of instantaneous flows of the physical values of these variables or *rates* between the levels in each network. In addition to these physical values, each level produces information representing those values with the result of an information network superimposed on the physical network and controlling it. He expands this notion as follows:

> The industrial system . . . is a very complex multi-loop and interconnected system. . . . Decisions are made at multiple points throughout the system. Each resulting action generates information that can be used at several but not all decision points. This structure of cascaded and interconnected information-feedback loops, when taken together, describes the industrial system. Within a company, the decision points extend from the shipping room and the stock clerk to the board of directors.[13]
>
> The interlocking network of information channels emerges at various points to control physical processes such as the hiring of employees, the building of factories, and the production of goods. Every action point in the system is backed up by a local decision point whose information sources reach into other parts of the organization and the surrounding environment.[14]

Forrester viewed management in terms of the sequence *information-decision-action,* with the decision-making process as a response to the gap between the objectives of the organization and its actual progress toward the accomplishment of these objectives.

Thus, industrial dynamics views organizations from a control perspective. It is intended mostly as a method of designing organizational policies. Nevertheless, industrial dynamics is a useful framework for information systems, management accounting in particular, in several ways:

1. It places information as an explicit and integral part of organizational decision making.
2. The information's function is to represent the physical values of the levels of various activities and entities in the organization.
3. It emphasizes the identification of decision points, objectives and information requirements.

4.5 DEARDEN FRAMEWORK

Dearden observes that the concept of a single information system is "too large and all-encompassing to be a meaningful and useful classification."[15] He suggests instead to break down the systems and data processing activities both horizontally and vertically. Horizontally, systems activities can be classified by the type of work performed; vertically, systems activities can be classified by the kind of information handled.

The horizontal classification includes three stages: systems specification, data processing implementation, and programming. These tasks are assumed to be different and should be treated differently. Systems specification should be decentralized to operating management or users because they have the best knowledge and capabilities required to determine what information should be provided by the system. Data processing implementation can and should be centralized because it improves the economics of integration of the data processing requirements, and should also be controlled by staff specialists because knowledge of equipment and data requirement is the primary requirement. Programming as a process of converting flow charts to working programs lends itself best to centralization. Dearden gives the following three reasons:

1. Programming is more economically accomplished on a centralized basis.
2. Writing business programs requires a special knowledge of equipment and programming languages, and there is practically no difference in the skills required to program the different systems.
3. Management must delegate the task of programming to someone, and it makes little difference whether it is a staff unit or a department reporting directly to the manager.[16]

The vertical classification is based on the presence of three major information systems in a typical company, and a varying and indefinite number of minor systems.

The major information systems include financial, personnel, and logistics. The basis of the financial system is the flow of dollars through the organization.[17] The personnel system is concerned with the flow of information about people working in the organization. It is assumed to be administered by the industrial relations officer. Finally, the logistics system is concerned with information about the physical flow of goods through an organization covering procurement, production, and distribution. Several separate logistic systems may be found in any one company. Dearden associates the financial system with Anthony's category of management control, and logistics system with operational control.

The minor systems, defined as those confined to a limited part of the organization, include mainly marketing, research and development, strategic planning, and executive observation. Some of these may be integrated to the three major systems or left separate.

Dearden finally proposes a generalized organization chart for systems and data processing based on the vertical and horizontal classification just described. Such a structure is illustrated in Exhibit 4.3.

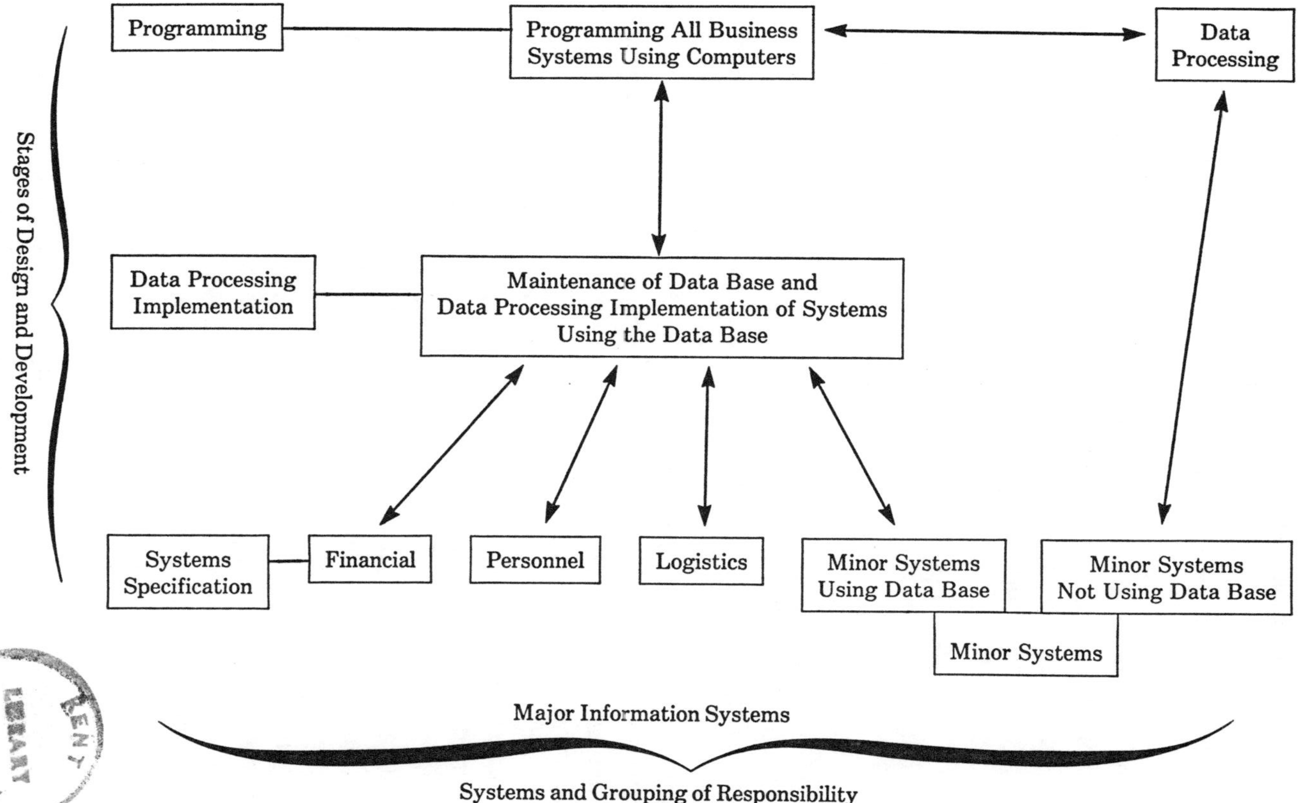

Exhibit 4.3 Dearden framework

4.6 BLUMENTHAL FRAMEWORK

Blumenthal presented his framework as a synthesis of the three concepts of information-decision-action suggested by Forrester, programmed and nonprogrammed decisions suggested by Simon, and the hierarchy of planning and control suggested by Anthony.[18] His major concern is the lack of consistent and uniformly applied approaches to the integration of related systems into larger entities of appropriate scope.

He starts with the activity center as being one of the basic organizational units in an organization under the common and direct supervision of a first-line manager. These activity centers are grouped into larger and complex organizational units known as decision centers, functional units, and management control centers. A decision center is defined as one or more management level people who either prescribe the decision rules or make the decisions for the activity centers. A functional unit is an activity center and its decision center. A management control center is one or more management people together with their supporting staff which acts as a decision center for a group of functional units or for a group of subordinate management control centers. The actions, carried by the same or different functional units, which regulate the inflow or outflow to or from sequences of levels as a group form an *operational function*.

Each of these organizational units may constitute groups to execute operational functions as action subsystems, decision subsystems, and information subsystems. The organization subsystems, the operational functions, and various modules constitute the main foundations of a management information system. Hence, a management information system is viewed as an operational function whose functional units are information subsystems of other operational functions. The modules are either operational or management control modules. An operational control module is viewed as that part of an information subsystem supporting the functional units of an operational function. A management control module is that part of an information subsystem supporting the management control centers of an operational function. Blumenthal concludes that a management information system is alternatively definable as an operational function whose parts are the management control modules and operational control modules of other operational functions.[19]

Blumenthal's framework has implications for management accounting. It advocates that the design and planning of any information system, including management accounting, be based on fundamental principles which refer to the effective use of systems resources, efficiency in systems life and performance, and organizational changes. The process advocated to ensure this objective consists of: (1) grouping the most elementary operational activities into identifiable and separate organizational units, (2) linking these activity centers to decision centers to form functional units, and (3) defining different modules (operational control module, management control module) as the basic components of the information system. This implies that both planning and control will take place at two levels: (1) operational planning and control for the operational, repetitive activities of the functional units; and (2) management planning and control for the operational functions.

4.7 CONCLUSIONS

A framework is needed in which to position where management accounting is now and the direction in which it can move in terms of determining the needed information, the type of decisions taken and decision centers, and defining the role of management accounting in decision making. Although such a framework has not been explicitly formulated, several conceptual frameworks for viewing information systems in general have been presented in the literature. These are, respectively, the

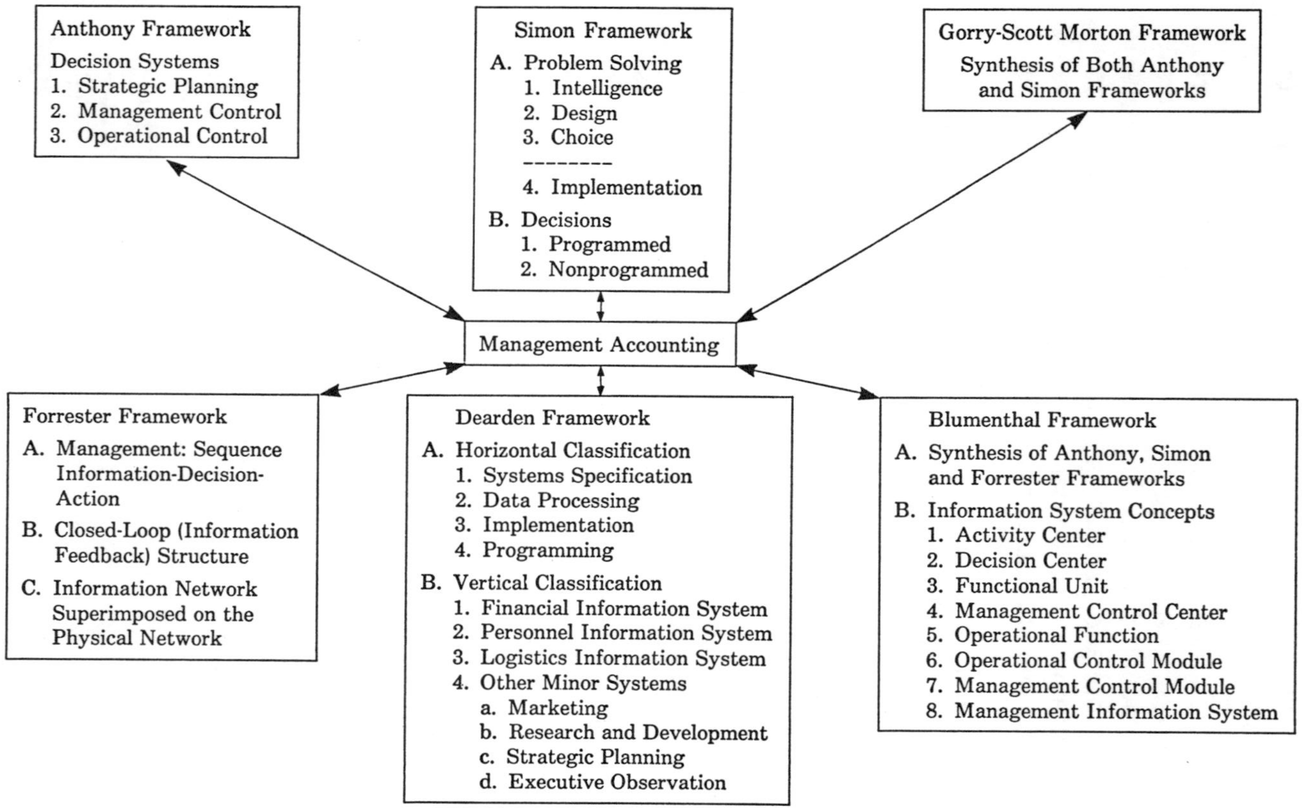

Exhibit 4.4 The decisional foundations of management accounting

Anthony framework, the Simon framework, the Gorry-Scott Morton framework, the Dearden framework, the Forrester framework, and the Blumenthal framework. As shown in Exhibit 4.4, these frameworks constitute the decisional foundations of management accounting by providing the basis for making resource allocation decisions about information systems, in general, and management accounting, in particular. They suggest the types of information needed for different categories of decisions and decision centers.

ENDNOTES

1. R. N. Anthony, *Planning and Control Systems: A Framework for Analysis* (Cambridge, Mass.: Harvard University Graduate School of Business Administration, Studies in Management Control, 1965).
2. Ibid., p. 24.
3. Ibid., p. 27.
4. Ibid., p. 69.
5. H. A. Simon, *The New Science of Management Decision* (New York: Harper and Row, 1960).
6. Ibid., pp. 5–6.
7. G. A. Gorry and M. S. Scott Morton, "A Framework for Management Information Systems," *Sloan Management Review* (Fall 1971): 55–70.
8. Henry C. Lucas, Jr.; Kenneth W. Clowes; and Robert B. Kaplan, "Frameworks for Information Systems," *INFOR* (October 1974): 251.
9. Gorry and Morton, "A Framework for Management Information Systems," p. 67.
10. Ibid., p. 68.
11. P. G. Keen and M. S. Scott Morton, *Decision Support Systems,* Addison-Wesley Series on Decision Support, (Reading, Mass.: Addison-Wesley Publishing Company, Inc., 1978), pp. 92–93.
12. J. W. Forrester, *Industrial Dynamics* (Cambridge, Mass.: M.I.T. Press, 1961).

13. Ibid., p. 94.
14. Ibid.
15. John Dearden, "How to Organize Information Systems," *Harvard Business Review* (March-April 1965): 66.
16. Ibid., p. 69.
17. It is assumed to be administered by the controller.
18. Sherman C. Blumenthal, *Management Information Systems: A Framework for Planning and Development* (Englewood Cliffs, N.J.: Prentice-Hall, Inc., 1969).
19. Ibid., p. 36.

BIBLIOGRAPHY

Ansoff, H. I. "Managerial Problem Solving." *Journal of Business Policy* (August 1971): 3–20.

Anthony, R. N. *Planning and Control Systems: A Framework for Analysis*. Cambridge, Mass: Harvard University Graduate School of Business Administration, Studies in Management Control, 1965.

Blumenthal, Sherman C. *Management Information Systems: A Framework for Planning and Development*. Englewood Cliffs, N.J.: Prentice-Hall, Inc., 1969.

Davis, Gordon B. *Management Information Systems: Conceptual Foundations, Structure and Development*. New York: McGraw-Hill Book Company, 1974.

Dearden, John. "How to Organize Information Systems." *Harvard Business Review* (March-April 1965): 65–73.

Ein Dor, Phillip, and Segev, Eli. *Managing Management Information Systems*. Lexington, Mass.: Lexington Books, 1978.

Forrester, J. W. *Industrial Dynamics*. Cambridge, Mass.: M.I.T. Press, 1961.

Gorry, G. A., and Morton, M. S. Scott. "A Framework for Management Information Systems." *Sloan Management Review* (Fall 1971): 55–70.

Hurtubise, Rolland. "La Conception des Systèmes d'Information: Un Cadre Conceptuel Global." *INFOR* (October 1978): 253–275.

Keen, P. G., and Morton, M. S. Scott. *Decision Support Systems.* (Addison-Wesley Series on Decision Support) Reading, Mass.: Addison-Wesley Publishing Company, Inc., 1978.

Lucas, Henry C., Jr.; Clowes, Kenneth W.; and Kaplan, Robert B. "Frameworks for Information Systems." *INFOR* (October 1974): 245–260.

Simon, H. A. *The New Science of Management Decision.* New York: Harper and Row, 1960.

Chapter 5

CONCLUSIONS

Various authors have criticized the limited scope generally given to management accounting. Anton points this out:

> Generally, managerial accounting has taken the following forms: (1) *Ad Hoc* approaches to single-instance decision situations simplified to involve only one or two variables, for example, make or buy decisions, (2) an expansion of cost accounting technique, e.g., cost planning and control, and (3) a more or less conventional approach to budgetary planning and control.[1]
>
> Managerial accounting has . . . addressed itself mainly to the problems of sub-optimization, and has largely worked outside the scheme of the "continuous *data-gathering*" system. It is rather obvious that this has been due largely to the fact that present accounting *systems* do not provide adequate structure to enable the gathering of enough pertinent managerial data from routine accounting records.[2]

This lack of adequate structure is mainly due to the failure to recognize the conceptual foundations of management accounting as a guide for the development and evaluation of management accounting techniques. As pointed out in this book, management accounting rests on accounting, organizational, behavioral, and decisional foundations. The incorporation of these foundations in management accounting will provide the adequate structure that will enable the gathering of enough pertinent managerial data for internal problem solving.

The accounting foundations include basic and secondary objectives, qualitative characteristics, and concepts as an accounting conceptual framework within which techniques may be evaluated. Management accounting techniques will be judged in terms of their conformity to this "emerging management accounting theoretical structure."

The organizational foundations include the elements of organizational structure most prevalent and essential to a proper functioning of a management accounting system and the theories of organization essential to an identification of the significant elements which approximate the patterning and order in organizations. They define the role and the scope of management accounting in the organization and the techniques, approaches, and philosophies it may espouse in order to provide adequate services to the organization.

The behavioral foundations include various concepts; namely, the objective function in management accounting, motivation theories, and models of decision making, which identify factors and situations that influence the individual behavior and performance, and suggest avenues for management accounting to adapt its services.

The decisional foundations include the frameworks for determining the needed information, the type of decisions taken and decision centers, and for defining the role of management accounting in decision making.

These conclusions point to the possibility of formulating a model of the nature, elements, and determinants of the conceptual foundations of management accounting. Such a model would represent a first step toward the development of a combinatorial theory of management accounting. The model is shown schematically in Exhibit 5.1. It attempts to synthesize or integrate various variables which explain the nature and determinants of the conceptual foundations of management accounting. Its main purposes are to identify all the variables or "elements of foundations" which purport to explain the scope and conduct of management accounting in a given organization.

More explicitly, the scope and conduct of management accounting in a given organization rests on four conceptual foundations: (1) accounting, (2) organizational, (3) behavioral, and (4) decisional foundations. Management accounting systems will differ from one another on the basis of the extent of appreciation and the incorporation of these foundations, their determinants, and their elements in the design of the system.

The model shows also that each of these foundations may be characterized by appropriate determinants. Hence, the accounting foundations are determined by the extent to which

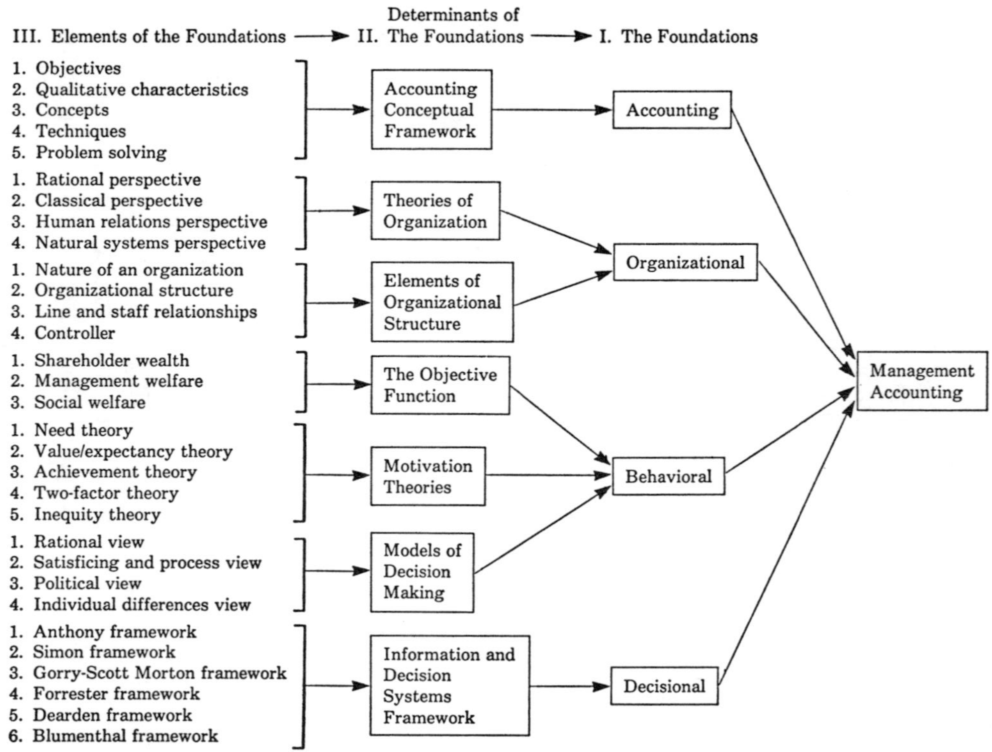

Exhibit 5.1 Emerging combinatorial theory of management accounting

management accounting techniques are derived from an accounting conceptual framework. The organizational foundations are determined by the theories of organization and the elements of organizational structure. The behavioral foundations are determined by the objective function, the motivation theories, and the models of decision making. The decisional foundations are determined by the information and decision system frameworks.

Each of the determinants of the conceptual foundations depend on the set of variables or elements of the foundations, which will characterize by their implementation the resulting management accounting system. Hence, the accounting conceptual framework will depend on the particular objectives, qualitative characteristics, and concepts used to justify and derive management accounting techniques. The theories of organization include the choice among the rational perspective, the classical perspective, the human relations perspective, and the natural systems perspective. The elements of organizational structure include the nature of an organization, the type of organizational client, the line and staff relationships, and the functions of the controller in the organization. The motivation theories include the need theory, the value/expectancy theory, the achievement theory, the two-factor theory, and the inequity theory. The models of decision making include the rational view, the satisficing and process-oriented view, the political view, and the individual differences view. Finally, the information and decision system frameworks include the Anthony framework, the Simon framework, the Gorry-Scott Morton framework, the Dearden framework, and the Blumenthal framework.

The model presented in Exhibit 5.1 is intended as a first step toward a combinatorial theory of management accounting. This theory would have relevance to accounting's objective of designing an efficient management accounting system which would serve management in all the aspects of internal decision making.

ENDNOTES

1. Hector R. Anton, "Activity Analysis of the Firm: A Theoretical Approach to Accounting (Systems) Development," *Lüketaloudellinen Aikakauskirja* (*The Journal of Business Economics*), Helsinki, IV (1961): pp. 290–305. Also, H. R. Anton, and P. Firmin, eds. *Contemporary Issues in Cost Accounting* (Boston: Houghton Mifflin Co., 1966), p. 293.
2. Hector R. Anton, "Some Implications of Information Theory for Business Organizations," Working Paper No. 49, Center for Research in Management Science, University of California, Berkeley 1962, Published in *Revista Internazionale Di Scienze Economiche E Commerciale,* (Milan, IX, 1962), p. 3.

INDEX